I0145694

Dragonfly Faith

Yada God with Me
Book One

Rhoda Fegan

ISBN 978-0-9862268-1-6

© Copyright 2022 by
Rhoda Fegan
All Rights Reserved

Contents

CHAPTER TWO

CHAPTER THREE

CHAPTER FOUR
The Trinity Calling

CONCLUSION
Life and Death

Preface
Yada God with Me

Have you ever heard the Hebrew word yada? In English, a single yada refers to talk. In Hebrew, yada means "intimate knowing." A deeper meaning for yada is a covenant relationship. Dragonfly faith is both. It is God talking to us to share His wisdom and love, and God wanting a meaningful and personal relationship with us, His creation.

Dragonfly faith is a place for you to read what God has been sharing with me for many years. I want you to see how God has revealed Himself in these random written pieces that I consider gifts from Him. I hope you feel His presence when you read His love notes.

Some of the pieces are simple and some more sophisticated than could come from my heart alone. It is indeed the Holy Spirit teaching me, inspiring me, growing me, and loving you through these spiritual food offerings. This book is God touching our lives where we strengthen our unity with God and each other. We please God by acknowledging His touch.

Settle back, relax, breathe God in and listen, for He is talking so we can yada Him.

Dedication

*Dedicated to the Trinity, Father Abba, Jesus Our Savior,
and the Holy Spirit, our ever present Helper.
To the Great Three in One who created us for a purpose.*

May all those who read these pieces glory in You and all that You do for Your children. May we never disappoint but when we do thank you for hearing our confession, forgiving, and forgetting our sin against You. Your world without end. Forever and always, Amen.

Introduction

Dragonflies, butterflies, and hummingbirds captured my attention years ago, and have become a part of the decoration in my home, and this wasn't lost on my husband, John. About ten days after his funeral on May 14, 2014, I received an artificial flower arrangement. The silk flowers were held in a container designed by Marjolein Bastian and the insert says, "In memories, flowers of HAPPINESS bloom through all the seasons of our LIVES." Amongst the flowers is a glass hummingbird with movable wings, a cloth bejeweled butterfly, and a dragonfly attached to a sphere that glows at night from the light it absorbs. I have since added a soft white bunny to the base of the container. The DAV support volunteer who delivered it said John had picked out everything for it and called her a few weeks before his death to remind her of her promise to deliver it to me. No amount of decluttering and downsizing will ever see it off of my great-grandmother Smith's library desk.

I am still stunned by his gift, but more I am stunned by the number of dragonflies I have seen since his death, starting in our own front yard that is at a fair distance from any water. I see them quite often when I am out. The summer of 2017, I sat in my car in a hospital parking lot with my daughter's three children while she had a follow-up appointment for her damaged driving foot. I watched four dragonflies dance around the parked cars in front of me, and one came up to the glass directly across from me, hovered, studied me for a while, then as if satisfied flew back to the other dragonflies. They remained in the parking lot until just before we left.

For me, the dragonflies carry a message from the man who shared my life from our meeting just before my seventeenth birthday until his death, including forty-one years of marriage. His message with God's cooperation is clear. He is healed now and waiting, but still interested in me.

Dragonflies have been around since prehistoric times and preserved remains of these winged insects have two-foot wingspans. By adaptation God preserved them to the lovely insects, dragonflies and damselflies, that we have today, and I am grateful that they are palm-size now. They are amazing, adaptable, but not adoptable. I have found many pieces about dragonflies and about the dragonfly to explain death, the first I found was by Doris Stickney.[1] I have adapted it for my book.

The Dragonfly

"Once, in a little pond, in the muddy water under the lily pads, there lived a community of water beetles. They lived a simple life in the pond with few disturbances and interruptions.

Occasionally, sadness would come to the community when one of the beetles would climb the stem of a lily pad never to be seen again. They knew when this happened that their friend was dead, gone forever.

Then, one day, a certain beetle felt the irresistible urge to climb up a stem. However, he was determined that he would not leave forever. He would come back and tell his friends what he had found at the top.

When he reached the top of the surface of the lily pad, he was tired, the sun felt so warm, that he took a nap. As he slept, his body changed and when he awoke, he had turned into a beautiful blue-tailed dragonfly with broad wings designed to fly.

He soared and saw the beauty of a whole new world, a far superior life than what he had known.

Then he remembered his friends and knew they thought him dead, so he tried to go back. **He wanted to tell them that he was more alive than he had ever been, and that his life had been fulfilled, not ended.**

But his new body could not go back to its former life, so he could not tell his friends the good news of his new body and his new life. But now he knew that they would too someday know what he now knew. So, he took to his wings and flew off to enjoy his joyous new life!"

Father, You put eternity into our hearts, so death is not the end, but just the close of the elementary days of our lives. Just like a water beetle that can live up to six years in its water phase before it becomes a dragonfly; just like butterflies who have their pre-life as caterpillars before they gain wings; so, we Your children live a pre-life as fragile human beings in temporary bodies before we take up our glorified eternal bodies. We are, Father, eternal beings living in earth suits, living our earthly days in You, until it's time to take the transforming step to our joyous new life! Death is but a step, for Jesus claimed victory over death and removed its sting. Thank you, Trinity, for rescuing and restoring up to Your original plan. By Your love and power, Father, Jesus, and the Holy Spirit. Amen.

Chapter One

Good Friday Offerings

This book is an attempt to bring the pieces together that God has given me as an act of gratitude, praise, and worship. One of the earliest pieces I found, Jesus, is in this chapter. It appears to have been written, printed, and never saved. I was tempted to leave it out, but Jesus is worthy of all our praise. Most of these pieces have only been seen by family members and a few friends from time to time. You should know that when I write my two favorite keys are backspace and delete; and I sometimes never seem to finish editing. I think God's Spirit likes spending the extra time with me. Whereas some of these pieces are simple, some complex, the newest pieces are Biblical Historical Pieces. Most surprise me but all nourish me. It is a smorgasbord! Try writing for yourself.

I have written every Good Friday for most of my adult life. I have placed some of the pieces I was given on those days in other chapters but these I left here because of their message. Look for the other pieces and see my Good Fridays, find the Holy Spirit, and pause for a chat. Most of the pieces end in a prayer, a time for me to talk to God. Some come with an explanation and are at times a glimpse of my life like a journal.

Peter speaks about the transfiguration of Jesus Christ on Mount Tabor witnessed by His disciples John, James, and himself. Clearly, these pieces acknowledge all that I believe and my willingness to write it down and to continue to grow spiritually through these efforts. Although not an eyewitness, I am through the power of the Trinity a heart witness to Their sovereignty, love, consistency and continuity, their history and future with Their creation, mankind.

For we did not follow cleverly devised tales when we made known to you the power and coming of our LORD Jesus Christ, but we were eyewitnesses of His majesty. For when He received honor and glory from God the Father, such a declaration as this was made to Him by the Majestic Glory: **"This is My beloved Son with whom I am well pleased."** *— and we ourselves heard this declaration made from heaven when we were with Him on the holy mountain. 2 Peter 1:16-18*

Resurrection

Crushed. Broken. He bleeds. He is dying.
Renewed. Revived. He breathes. He breathes! He is living.

Sinful. Lost. I am separated. I am dying.
Ashamed. Contrite. I am pardoned. I am living.

Renewed. Alive. I live fulfilled to sing His praises.
My death and resurrection will be in Him. I'll live throughout the ages.

I first started to write from my spirit Good Friday April 1, 1988, my husband John's birthday. Don't do any math but realize it was before the internet, e-mail, Facebook, and blogs.

I was driving to work that Good Friday thinking about my maternal grandmother, Ida Agnes Weidner, Born March 10,1897 and Home with our LORD July 7, 1987, as it was my first Easter with her in eternity. Growing up she was the third adult in our household. She was the stay at home "mom" for four of her eleven grandchildren. She traditionally spent the hours of Christ's crucifixion in prayer and meditation each Good Friday, and we could only interrupt her if someone was bleeding or dying. So, yes, we learned to respect her Good Friday tradition.

So, I prayed to thank God for her legacy of faith and the tremendous gift of Christ's obedience that bought my salvation. Then I wrote the draft of Resurrection on the back of a yellow McDonald's napkin at red lights as I drove to work! I will never claim to be a poet. I never wrote while driving again, and never worked another Good Friday. And, God has met with me every Good Friday since and many other days as well. This piece is very simple, and I love it as much as those that are more complex. The variety of the pieces that I created from the Holy Spirit touches me, and so I know heaven can never be boring.

Thank you, Father for meeting with me and giving me this love note, and all the many more that have come over the years. Grandma prayed during Your hours of crucifixion, but the Holy Spirit has met with me and gives me writings. Now seems to be the time to share them with Your other earth-bound children. They have been food for my soul and my joy—for when I write I feel You near. Let Your words touch others as they have touched and fed me. Thank you, Jesus for loving me and dying to restore me to my birthright as God's beloved daughter. By Jesus' precious blood. Amen and love from your daughter, Rhoda.

Jesus

Sweet Baby Jesus Mary held in arms.
Sweet Baby Jesus who grew up so strong.

Sweet young Child Jesus who fashioned wood with His hands.
Sweet young Child Jesus who brought healing with His hands.

Sweet LORD Jesus who confounded the elders and the priests.
Sweet LORD Jesus who came to shepherd His lost sheep.

Holy LORD Jesus who turned water into wine.
Holy LORD Jesus who died for all mankind.

Holy LORD Jesus crucified to pay the price.
Holy LORD Jesus sacrificed to give me life.

Holy LORD Jesus I praise Your name.
Holy LORD Jesus I remember Your pain.

Unknown Good Friday

Father, this reminds me that Your love and grace doesn't depend on me remembering the day, time, or year because You are always with me. I am reminded of the words of Pastor Phil Jones. He said, "We don't need You every hour, because we have You every hour." Jesus died to be my advocate at Your throne, and I want no other, because Christ dying for me showed me that no One would ever love me more; forgive me more, be more gracious or kind, would ever forget more, nor advocate better for me. There aren't enough words to offer enough praise! Thank you, LORD Jesus. Amen.

Gift

Only one gift of value I have.
Only one gift of value to give.
Only one gift bought at a great price.
Only the gift of Christ's sacrifice.

Take from my hand the gift of God's love.
Take from my hand the gift of God's son.
Take from my hand the gift prepared for you.
Take from my hand the gift that will make you new.

Take from my hand the gift of the Holy Spirit.
Take from my hand the gift Christ promised you.
The Holy Spirit will come and dwell within your heart.
You will have them to guide you safely to eternity.

Yours is the gift of great value
offered to you this day.
Yours the gift of great value
that will come to you when you pray.

Abba, Jesus, Holy Spirit. This is one of the smaller pieces You have gifted to me. They are not just words on paper, but praise, and You are welcomed here. These pieces are food for my soul, and I want to share them now. Use them to nourish and inspire others. There is a storyteller and writer in many others. Let these pieces encourage them as they have me. Let them feel Your presence and place the desire in their hearts to always want to feel Your presence around and in them. Thank you, Abba, for letting each of us breathe You in; look for the joy in each day, to follow hard after You, and offer our praise anytime. Thank you for the room You have prepared for each of us in Your Eternal Kingdom. Forever and ever, Abba, Jesus, and the Holy Spirit. Amen.

Would you be so...

Would you be so...
If tomorrow the birds would stop their singing;
If tomorrow the flowers would stop blooming?

Would you be so...
If today you knew you were appointed to die;
If today you knew your brother in a grave would lie?

Would you be so...
If yesterday you understood the sacrifice;
If yesterday you understood the one called Jesus Christ?

August 23, 1992

Abba, my earliest writings were often quite simple, and I would try to rhyme them. They spoke truth to me and resonated with me then, and still. It is all about You, Abba, Jesus, My Savior, and the Holy Spirit. Use these words as You will. They are Your words. I thank you, for choosing me and leading me to find You early in my life. By the sacrifice of Jesus, I come, and I surrender my all to You. Amen.

Sacrificed

Impaled upon a rough-hewed cross You were too weak to carry
You suffered agony like no other.
Nailed through feet and hands to die You refused all pain relief
And called upon a trusted friend to care for Your mother.

Sinless yet being crucified with the sin of all mankind upon your shoulders
You gave pardon to another, so he could enter Paradise.
Suspended between heaven and earth You wore a crown of thorns
and endured the greatest agony when the Father forsook you as you paid the required price.

Betrayed, accursed, condemned, beaten, tormented, tortured,
Mocked, nailed to an old-rugged cross,
You were the only holy acceptable sacrifice.

Resurrected, Glorified Holy Lamb of God You are the LORD of Glory,
LORD of Love, LORD of Life and Light and I thank You
For the gift of eternal life with You in Paradise.

April 5, 1996

Father, Good Friday and Easter Sunday have always held greater importance in me than Christmas. Perhaps because You started meeting me on Good Fridays and sharing the day, Your Holy Spirit, Your Words, and Your Heart with me. Surely, it is because of all Jesus suffered for me. Christmas is a holiday set aside worldwide in many countries for festivities that leave You out, but Good Friday is just a footnote on the calendar. It is not commercialized, but Satan has tried to mask the importance of Good Friday by emphasizing Easter with the Easter bunny. Thank you for keeping my focus on You and Christ's sacrifice for me. Amen.

February 2020: I like my granddaughter, Abbi's, Sunday School class creation of the three crosses on Golgotha's hill. There is a lamb glued to the middle cross and an adult wrote this caption on it, "It is about the Lamb, not the Easter bunny." To this I say Amen. Thank you, Jesus, for not only coming, but fulfilling the plan of salvation and restoration, for me and mine, and the people of Your world without end. Glory and Honor and my love. Amen.

Other Sacrifices

The LORD talked with me today when I went to Him in prayer to thank Him for Easter.

"It's Good Friday, LORD. Thank you for Your Sacrifice."

"What sacrifice?"

"Why your crucifixion, LORD? Without it I wouldn't have forgiveness and eternal life."

"Your welcome," was the gentle reply.

Yet, I heard something more in His answer, so I paused to ask, "What is it, LORD?"

"There were other sacrifices, my child."

"Other sacrifices, LORD?" My mind raced to imagine what more the LORD would say.

**"Before the world was, my Father and I shared glory and We talked face to face.
Then, one day my Father said, "It is time."
And I replied. "I know the plan Father if it is possible, let this cup pass from Me,
yet not as I will, but as You will."**
**"All heaven waited, hoping with Me that there was another way to bring the gift of salvation to mankind,
but my Father's holiness could only accept the full designated price.
My Father lovingly laid His hand on Mine. I answered His love for you the only way I could."
"My Father, if this cup cannot pass away unless I drink it then, I will obey."
"Then, I stood and the angels before the throne parted.
I left the presence of My Father and heaven that day to become the infant Christ Child born of Mary."**

The import of what He had shared with me weighed heavily upon me and I cried out my praise to Him.
"Oh, Master, how could You have left heaven,
The shared glory of being with Your Father and the Holy Spirit,
Left being able to commune with Them face to face for such as I?"

**"My beloved child, how could I not? I loved You even as My Father and Spirit did.
His Holiness required that I pay the price of Your redemption and I paid it willingly out of Our love for You."**

My tear stained face lifted into the light of His love.
"Thank you, LORD, for sacrificing Heaven and Your relationship in the Trinity for me."
I paused for a moment, dreading to ask more,
But the Spirit living in me gave me the courage to ask, "Is there more, LORD."

**"Indeed child. Once in human form, I came to understand what being human meant.
Not only did I face temptations more than any man, but I learned to love in human terms.
Mary, My mother, was so beautiful and loving, and Joseph was strong and kind
and taught Me to be a skillful carpenter. I had brothers and sisters too.
Yet, the time came when I had to leave them to begin My ministry."**

"So, You left home and family for me too, LORD?"

"Yes, for there was no other way for Me to prepare others to teach the Truth."

I trembled wondering if I could give up home or family
And could only say "Thank you," in a weak small voice.
The Spirit inside me then asked the LORD to continue when I couldn't ask on my own.

"My Father gave Me twelve strong men. You know them as My disciples.
There were those that night whose first concern were their places in heaven,
And I warned Peter that Satan would sift him.
Thomas had been willing to die with Me earlier at Bethany should the need have come,
When I went to raise My friend, Lazarus, from his grave.
One of them betrayed Me, even though I loved him.
Peter thought he was brave enough to die with Me that night, he defended Me with his sword,
yet ran away in fear. My sheep all left Me in fear, so I had to face the cross alone.
I remember the sadness in Peter when he had denied Me for the third time
Before the rooster crowed the day as I looked into his eyes.
Yet, except for Judas, they genuinely loved Me,
And I built My church on Peter and the others who followed Me.
I showed Myself to them after My resurrection that first Easter morning
And turned their mourning into joy and understanding.
They are eyewitnesses to the completion of My Father's plan."

As the LORD paused, I saw His betrayal, false trail,
His unmerciful beatings that left Him injured beyond recognition,
And finally, I saw His crucifixion.
And just as my soul could no longer endure facing His agony,
The LORD's voice came once again to my ears.
"I gave up My life, leaving behind My family, friends, and followers.
They could not understand that it was a part of the plan."

A voice then reached my ears that I barely perceived as my own.
"So, you gave up everything on earth that You held dear to die on the cross for me?
How can I praise You enough for all You sacrificed to give me life, LORD?
There are no words, there's not enough tears to say thank you, LORD."

Once again, the LORD's voice came to comfort me.
"When in the time to come, You stand beside Me in the presence of My Father and I can say,
"Father, this is My good and faithful servant." It will be enough for all eternity."

My wretched spirit quieted within me.
And I looked at the cross from Jesus' side.
Another voice was heard, and it was like thunder,
Yet gentle and did not cause me any fear, and I understood.

"This is My Beloved Son, in whom I am well pleased. Take your rest in Him."

The Spirit praying with me, and I said, "Amen."

Easter 1997

Father, this piece came late in the day. I had no thoughts of what I would write before the day started and nothing seemed to be coming. It was after three in the afternoon, and I got in my car and drove away from my home and desk and prayed. Then, You gave this to me. Thank you, Jesus, for giving up heaven for me, Your family, Your disciples, Your human life for me. I saw how Your divine nature and humanity made this possible for You to do for the likes of me. Your knowledge of what You would be returning to in Heaven, Your long-awaited reunion with Your Father and the Holy Spirit, and Your plan for all those who would believe and be with You for all eternity made the impossible for You possible. Thank you, Jesus, for all You sacrificed. Eternal praise. Amen.

Were You There?

There's an old gospel song that asks, "Were you there when they crucified my LORD?"
In my spirit these past few weeks as I've contemplated the events of this holy season,
I heard the same question and have tried to answer it.

There is no doubt many who hear this song would have it resonate with them.
Many educated people would scoff and state that the individuals who placed Christ on the cross,
Who stood watch at His death or died beside Him are long since dead.
Those living now could not have been there, and I recognize my place is in the present as well.
But the answer to the question is even still a resounding, "Yes."

Christ so fills my heart, my mind, and my spirit that I've no doubt that everything
He did and felt was done for my benefit.
He left heaven in obedience taking on mortal flesh.
How was He able to restrict Himself from glory and heaven for thirty three years for me?
In an age, when life was so much more cumbersome,
He experienced life and love of family and friends, and then gave them up.
He chose disciples knowing how their individual life experiences would unfold.
He loved men who could not stay vigil even while He prayed to the Father
For an alternative plan to His death.

Even while the agony of the weight of the brutality He faced,
the weight of our sin, and the cruel death of the cross was accepted by Him in prayer with His Father,
He loved His disciples, and all of us.
He loved those who betrayed His love and His trust as no other could.
What more could my loving Savior do, but to take on the frailty of flesh, love me, and die for me?
I stood in the shadow of the cross on that first Good Friday.
I, daughter of Christ, was there in my robe of sin,
As Jesus was nailed to the cross, so that He filled the gap between heaven and earth, heaven and me.
I was there, and the blood from His beaten, nailed, and slashed body fell on me, healed me,
And turned my garment white with the purity of His completed sacrifice.

I go there even now.
I travel the gap of time without even a blink of my eye each time I think of His life,
Ministry, death, and commission. I stand with the other women at the base of His cross
And agonize over my complicity in His suffering and His death.
I stand huddled at the base of His cross seeing and being touched by His agony
as God shrouds the earth in darkness and turns His face from His only begotten and beloved Son.
I am there as the essence of His life is released at His spoken command.
I am there when His sorely battered body is finally placed in Mary's open arms.
I see her cradle his beloved Head and remove the crown of thorns from His brow.
I watch as His body is wrapped and carefully laid in the borrowed tomb.

For me though, there is no wait to see the promise of His resurrection fulfilled,
Because I know the tomb that was borrowed was returned that first Easter morning.
I go there and see His empty shroud deserted on the rough rock ledge that no longer bears His weight
And I see His face cloth carefully folded and laid aside.
His carefully folded face cloth, the promise of His return.
I see the angels speak to the women and watch as Mary talks to her Beloved Teacher.
What a glorious first morning of salvation made real.
I was there when they crucified my LORD.
I was there when they laid Him in the tomb.

I stand before the tomb and see the stone is rolled away;
And that the borrowed tomb is empty except for Jesus' unnecessary burial cloths.
I still go there. Isn't that the hope of Easter, the joy of forgiveness, the gift of salvation,
And the richness and fullness of being among the chosen of God?

Easter
April 2, 1999

Father, I heard the question from this song and this answer came from me. How is it possible for my spirit to join with the Holy Spirit? I am grateful that it did and does. Thank you for meeting with me to celebrate Christ's death and resurrection, and the completion of Your Restoration plan. My praise, Father, Jesus, and the Holy Spirit. Amen.

Alive and Well

Eternal soul and living spirit bestowed at conception.
You were sent to dwell amongst the weeds and thorns in an earthly tent.
From the first trembling of the heart to beat did you not breathe?
Did you not draw comfort from the warmth of your nether world?

Did the beating of another heart and the voice that most often pierced the womb comfort you.
Did you not struggle against the confines of such a limited tent?
Even as the wee body grew to its full capacity were you
Not laced in too small a space?

When it wailed the displeasure of all babes cast into the world,
Did you not commune with the Creator?
Your sojourn on earth was new and fragile in such a small fleshy tent,
Did you not ask for His companionship throughout the journey?

Eternal soul and living spirit: did you speak to the mind of your newly fashioned tent?
Did you not instruct it to look for His will all along the way?
At the time of your union were you not the link between the Creator and the being,
And did you not plead with it to have its God-shape hollow filled by the Master?

How was the moment when the creature acknowledged the Creator,
And you could feel God inside of it and no longer at a distance?
Did you rejoice long, or did you quickly set to work to tear down any strongholds
Left that would-be barriers to the communion of the Holy Spirit?

Were you overwrought that the Son had been the required Sacrifice,
So that you and your earthly tent could live in harmony with the Father,
The Holy Spirit, and our LORD Jesus Christ?
The journey short or long had its valleys, but was each breath the sweeter
For the growing trust and faithfulness?

Eternal soul and spirit at the body's journey end did you yearn
To reach out and touch the Master's hand?
No longer confined in space and finite time did you soar into the heavens
With your angel guide?

Did you at last rejoice when you knelt at the Savior's feet?
How did the body glorified feel as Jesus stood beside you at the Judgment seat?
Did you momentarily weep when Christ showed the Father His nail scarred hands,
And said it was for you, His Child, that He suffered, bled, and died?

When did you see them, the other eternal souls and living spirits
That were the heritage of your earthly tent?
How joyful was your reunion with the loved ones you once held dear?
How was the welcome home party held for you in your heavenly home?

Clothed now in robes of righteousness purchased by Christ at such a price,
Did you gather with the other saints to sing Holy, Holy, Holy in His throne room?
Do you wait there even now in prayer for us to join you
When we at last escape our earthly confines?

When at last the shackles of weak or aging flesh have
Been removed and the weeds and thorns left behind,
We like Christ are not dead but home after the sojourns end.
Gone? Only from earthly eyes for the eternal eyes still see us as we are.
Alive and well for this is our Father's plan.

Easter
March 25, 2005

Father, I wrote this to celebrate the death of one of our church members. I felt him not as dead, but certainly how he is forever, alive, and well. Sometimes when I write I learn how I feel or what I should believe. Thank you, Father, that he died but is not dead in You. You placed eternity in our hearts, because we are alive from the moment our hearts first start to beat. Our bodies die and are seeded to ash or ground, but our essence returns to You to live forever. It is my prayer that it is to reward and not judgment. The world You created will be restored and we will live with You forever. You alone are worthy of all glory and honor. Amen.

Dear Jesus

I am so in love with You, LORD and now declare it.
O LORD Jesus, before the world was created,
You shared glory with God, Our Father.
Angels bowed down to you in glad adoration.
You were God's Only Son, His delight before creation.

Sin entered the world through Adam and Eve.
Yet, in the fullness of time you came to earth as a baby.
Angels declared Your birth to a world trapped in darkness.
And You became our eternal light.
God affirmed His love for us on that night.

You are now my light, my love, my life.
My soul could be trapped in strife,
grief, concerns, any of life's sorrows.
Yet not, as these are life burdens that You carry for me each day,
As I seek the joy and comfort of being your child and offer praise.

God tested Abraham's faith when he called for Isaac to be sacrificed.
In obedience he journeyed forward to pay the price,
And placed his son upon an altar.
But, before the blade made its way into his tender flesh,
You substituted a perfect ram and gave this father and son rest.

When the children of Israel, left their Egyptian captivity,
All the firstborn of the land were to die that fateful night.
But the death angel passed over all the houses covered
In the blood of a perfect lamb and so God spared
Those animals, sons, and daughters.

When Cain killed his brother Abel,
His blood cried out for recognition and retribution.
You gave up your life on Calvary and Your blood
Paid for my redemption and forgiveness.
No other lamb was worthy to be the final sacrifice.

You crushed death and rose again.
And sit beside the Father as my Savior and Advocate.
Yet a little while and I will kneel at Your nail scarred feet,
And feel Your forgiving touch as Your nail scarred hands bid me rise.
Dressed in robes of white bought by Your blood, I will see Your glory with eternal eyes.

Easter 2006

Father, I feel love this Easter, but this is a strange love poem. Love though should be full or recognition for what Your Love sacrificed. Love should be grateful. Love should see the truth. Love should grow. My love, most Holy Father, Jesus Savior, and Holy Spirit. Amen.

Chisholm Bend Mill

There was no one around anymore who could tell stories about the old grist mill at Chisholm Bend.
It had been useless and abandoned for generations.
The whitewashed clapboards had been polished clean by the changing seasons, wind, snow, and rain.
The twister of '98 had removed some slate;
There were warped boards where windows used to peer out of the old building;
And much to its humiliation it bore the disrespect of a new generation of less than skilled graffiti artists.

The good earth around it had been fruitful in the way of cursed soil, so dead vegetation, barren young saplings,
And more mature barren trees rested in its shadow as witness to yet another winter just passing.
Only the old decaying water wheel creaked in obedience to its task
As it made each revolution capturing the energy of the water running past it,
But it was a joyless task as the grindstone had long since been disconnected.
It did still offer a bit of comfort and shelter to generations of field mice,
Rabbits and the like, and a few great birds of prey nested
In its hand-hewn beams away from gaps in the roof.
Neglect shamed the old proud mill, but the endless silence was far worse.
There had been a time when it resounded with life and was considered a favorable place to stop.

Yes, counted in eternal time, God's time,
It was only yesterday that neighbors had hauled wagons of grains through its massive doors,
And sales of crops were negotiated on the plank tongue and groove floors.
If you listened carefully you could still hear young men as they swapped tails of hunts and family,
And old men shared farming secrets, failures, and successes.
You could still smell the pipe tobacco that lingered after the smoker
Had headed out for home and the earth friendly smell of horse droppings.
You could watch as families gathered there to celebrate the fourth
And the harvests with tables laden with foods to share.
But no one came anymore.
Only the old mill heard the weather being discussed, plain gossip being shamefully repeated,
Births being cheered, and passing's being mourned while children played in the clearing and the creek.

There was yet another sun rising that greeted the old mill as the first clear spring day started.
Some men in sturdy trucks, modern day wagons, beat the vegetation down
As they made a path around the trees and came to a stop before the solid massive doors.
The old mill shuttered, and the boards creaked in misgiving as cutters
Were applied to break the rusted chain and keyless lock.
The hinges held as the doors were forced open against the ground
that had once been smooth and had allowed the doors to swing freely.
The creatures that hadn't already left fled and the mill wished it could depart too.
With large battery-operated lanterns, the men spread out to examine the interior of the building.
This day was a long time coming, but the mill stood proudly as it waited to hear the words –
Ruined, worthless, beyond repair, salvage and demolish.
It had served well, had its time in the sun, had lived, been abandoned, abused,
And suffered the pains of disease – time and neglect.
It deserved a noble end.

The group of men regrouped at the trucks and the old mill watched as they gestured.
It heard some of the words it had long feared – clear, salvage, and demolish.
But there were other words as well – solid, remodel, feature, and they just don't build them like this anymore.
It took months, really almost a year, but time no longer lingered uselessly for the old mill.
Each day bought it new life, new rooms, new purpose, and one day the old,
Refurbished wheel was put to use again, and its energy was converted to electricity
And the lights set aside the beams showed not an old, neglected mill but a new modern home.
Its exterior was now polished with a new metal roof, new paint,
And large windows that overlooked other smaller homes being built.
It was no longer alone but had neighbors.
There was a mom and dad, who deeply appreciated the beauty of the old
Blended with the new in the historic structure.
And there were two toddlers and a babe in arm who would be trained to appreciate
The legacy and who would keep it in trust for generations to follow.
The old mill was proud of its new position.
It once again provided shelter and comfort as a unique home as time passed over its little family.
How much are we like the old mill?

God gives each of us life and our days in the sun, but we don't even have to be old to be neglected,
Abused, abandoned, or labeled useless by man.
God never sees us as useless, unlovely, disabled, alien, ruined, or beyond hope.
Imperfect in our trespasses and sins, God loves us and calls to us.
Christ looking forward in time saw us and gave His life as full payment to cancel our debt of sin.
When we acknowledge our sin and seek His forgiveness,
He gives it along with the added gift of forgetfulness.
He forgives and forgets our sins.
No matter what our state when we seek God and He takes us into the comfort of His loving arms,
He labels us "His Children."
Then, like the old mill, our former state, our past, falls away and
We are renewed to live a new life in Him.
Then, we too have a legacy to pass forward to our children and grandchildren
For we can give them everything we own,
But if we don't give them the knowledge of God and His love,
Then we have given them nothing of value at all.

God's clock ticks in eternal time.
One day we will step out of these temporal dwellings, our earthly bodies,
To glorified immortal dwellings that will not know age, illness, or frailties.
The gift of Christ coming as a babe, dying as a very human man but very God,
Our Savior and LORD is complete,
But not fulfilled until we acknowledge and accept His sacrifice.
The Master Carpenter is at hand to take you as you are and renew you
Into what is useful and wanted for all eternity.
Choose life – eternal life in Christ Jesus.

Easter 2008

*"For I know the thoughts that I think toward you, says the L*ORD*, thoughts of peace and not of evil, to give you a future and a hope. Then you will call upon Me and go and pray to Me, and I will listen to you. And you will seek Me and find Me, when you search for Me with all your heart."* NKJV *Jeremiah 29:11-13*

Father, You know that my mind thought of this piece for almost a year before it found its way to paper. It took over six hours and John read it and asked, "It took you all day to write this?" I never told him that it took way longer. I go to a special place when I write, thank-you. My niece, Kimmy, saw it and called me about the personification of the mill. Surprised that I wrote it. This piece stands alone for that characteristic, but I pray a reader will find how it parallels us as living beings. It is one of my very favorite gifts, but then, Father, many are. Thank you for sharing this with me. Forever Father. Amen.

Sting

When I think of the time and conditions to which You came to our dark and despairing world, I am choked with raw emotions and tears; and I am overwhelmed by the depth of the darkness; the despair of the people, the great hopelessness of the time. There was so little then, and I have so much - a home with a furnace and central air; a job that provides more than we need; a family that knows to rely on You; and I live in a time where there is medicine and no certainty of death for young or old where treatments are available. There are laws now that hold back the cruelty of Your time; and I have not sold myself, my children, or grandchildren into servitude for food or shelter; nor have I been taken into slavery. Yet, this was the fullness of time, the right time, when You came to bring comfort, healing, and reparation between heaven and earth. You folded back time to restore the fellowship of man and God that was lost in the Garden of Eden with Adam and Eve's fall from grace.

I feel the heaviness of the day, the last supper with the men You loved pressing upon You; even then you thought of me and prayed for me and mine. I love that prayer. The spirit within me grieves knowing how troubled Your spirit had to have been when You handed Judas the dipped morsel. For You already knew what he had sold himself to do. I shiver in sorrow for the prayer time in Gethsemane when You wept alone accepting the cup the Father had given You to drink.

I picture the chaos in the garden, the fear, the betrayal, and one act of courage as Peter tried to defend You with his sword. One last miracle, when You restored the ear of the servant, Malchus, that Peter's sword had removed. Even in that moment, Your life on earth was about us, the people You had come to save. How did Malchus' life change in those few moments with You? Did he follow You that night? Did he become Your disciple? Will I meet him in heaven?

What a night Jesus! You were questioned and humiliated in the custody of the high priest, Caiaphas, and scourged by the Roman Governor, Pilate who had declared You innocent of any Roman law. It chills me to read that when Peter was identified as Your follower for the third time, he was so close that You turned to look at him. Was that sadness in Your eyes, or compassion for him? *"And Peter went outside and wept bitterly."* [1]

This brings tears to my eyes and my heart cringes. I feel for Peter. He wanted to be with You. He swallowed back his natural fear and crept close. How often he is criticized for this moment, along with his attempt to walk on the water. I can't criticize. Didn't he do more than I would have? Peter found Your forgiveness so long ago, yet are there times now when You look straight at me, when I have not spoken or acted inside Your will? Forgive me, LORD!

Then, there is Your painful struggle to carry Your cross to Golgotha. How quickly did Simon of Cyrene, who was forced to carry Your cross, shrink back away into the crowd when You came to the Place of a Skull? Or did Simon remain to witness Your crucifixion? Was he forever changed by being in Your presence?

The long hours on the cross – again I look back through the centuries to watch and be horrified by the torturous process of the crucifixion. I know this Roman execution process was about pain and suffocation, but You remained in control. You were Christ the Redeemer, and You had compassion on the thief who rebuked the second thief, who railed against You. I am glad that one chose to believe in You, yet, saddened by the second's choice, denial and loss for all eternity.

Then, the thief said to You, *"Remember me when You come to Your kingdom!"* And You answered him, ***"Truly I say to you, today you shall be with me in Paradise."*** Dying You still served and saved Him. [2]

Then noon came, *"And, it was now about the sixth hour (noon), and darkness fell over the whole land until the ninth hour, the sun being obscured, and the veil of the temple torn in two (top to bottom, not possible by human means). And You cried out with a loud voice, and said,* **"Father into thy hands I commit My spirit."** [3]

Then, You took Your last breath and gave up Your spirit having declared that the plan of salvation was finished. You laid down Your life for mine. Is this not proof of our immortality? Would You have died for us if there was only this life and then nothing? Oh, yes, we have fragile earth suits that we will exchange for glorified bodies designed to live in Paradise, but we will continue - we will be alive! And, for the thieves crucified with You, isn't that evidence that we all have a choice to make? Oh, dear friends and family choose Jesus!

What was the hardest part of all of this for You, LORD? The betrayal of Judas, one of Your own; Peter's denial; the torture, the pain, and humiliation; the weight of the sin of the world, my sin, upon Your own sinless nature; or was it the separation from Your Father? Mark tells us that at the ninth hour as the time of Your death was close, You cried to Your Father, **"My God, My God, why hast thou forsaken me?"** What kind of pain was that for You? I am frozen in sorrow for not only the depth of Your human suffering, but for this suffering. For hours on the cross, with the land unusually dark, You hung on a cross for me, and God in His Holiness couldn't extend Himself to look upon You, His only Son, because You had taken on my sin. Forgive me Jesus, forgive me. [4]

Triumphant resurrection Sunday – the earth felt You alive again! The massive stone no longer sealed Your tomb; the frightened guards had fled; and Your grave clothes lay untouched by any movement as You took up Your body again. Your face cloth was folded neatly; a sign at the time that the master of a household was not finished with dinner but was returning. Surely that is a sign to us that You are returning.

Then, You revealed Yourself to Your followers starting with Mary Magdalene at the tomb. The Bible tells us of how You appeared in a locked room to the assembly; later to Thomas who hadn't been in the room; how You walked along with two of Your disciples on the road to Emmaus and shared a pleasant interlude with them unawares until You blest and broke bread with them; and You made a meal on the beach for Your disciples and restored Peter to Yourself. Does this reveal then, LORD, what our new bodies will be able to do? You died for us out of such great love; returned and revealed to Your followers this great plan; and they passionately went out to reveal it to all who were lost. And, down through the centuries, despite threats, despite oppression, despite torture and death, Satan has not been able to stop You. So, I came to believe in You, but so many others refuse to accept You. Oh, precious LORD Jesus, I pray that they will come to accept You, before Your return.

But those events were not the beginning of Your human demonstration of Your divine and unconditional love for us. It started well before, and Your mother Mary, *"Mary kept all these things, and pondered them in her heart."* [5]

Mary and Joseph were totally human. Mary was a mere teen when Gabriel came to her and spoke to her of her election to be Your mother. Joseph was reasonably older, but it is evident that he cared for her and wanted no harm to befall her, but because of a divine dream took her as his wife and did not consummate their marriage until after You were born. I know the wonder of holding a newborn; amazed by the miracle of newborn life and the responsibility of the care of such a fragile creation. But Mary and Joseph were the parents of the hope of mankind, God incarnate.

Albert Barnes' commentary says this of Mary's pondering, "Here is a delicate and beautiful expression of the feelings of a mother. A "mother" forgets none of those things which occur respecting her children. Everything they do or suffer - everything that is said of them, is treasured up in her mind; and often she thinks of those things, and anxiously seeks what they may indicate respecting the future character and welfare of her child."

I can expect no less of Joseph. How did he father the son of God? If any human father feels the burden of rearing and protecting a child, how much greater was Joseph's burden? His job was to provide and to protect both mother and child. He had to find shelter for Mary to give birth, and You were born in the tower of the flock where sacrificial lambs were born. Like us though, Joseph and Mary were never alone. God was always there to guide them including communicating to Joseph through divine dreams.

As a mother, I can tell the stories of my children's births; I can relate stories of their childhoods; and tell you of their calls to salvation. But we know little of You as a child, but I can imagine you working with Joseph and being snuggled to sleep against Mary's breast. Moreover, I can imagine ordinary childhood moments and extraordinary events that would mirror the extraordinary events of Your years of ministry. How do you scold or punish God's child, or was it ever necessary?

We know the story of You staying behind in Jerusalem. Mary, like all mothers, asked, *"Son, why have You treated us like this? Your father and I have been anxiously searching for You."* And, unfettered by the concerns of a normal child separated from his parents for days, left behind in a strange city, you responded, **"Why were you searching for Me?' He asked. 'Didn't you know I had to be in My Father's house?'** But, as parents of this holy child, they didn't understand. Then, the Bible tells us, *"Then He went down to Nazareth with them and was obedient to them. But His mother treasured all these things in her heart. And Jesus grew in wisdom and stature, and in favor with God and men."* [6] Parenting is not an easy job. It is why so many fail, when they fail to include God in the nurturing and rearing process. Mary and Joseph didn't fail as evidenced by Your obedience to be the Lamb of our Salvation.

There is so much more to the moments of Your life, death, and resurrection that the Bible shares with us. I am moved by Your care for Your mother as she stands by Your cross. John tells us that when you saw Your mother and him standing nearby you said to her, **"Woman, behold, your son!"** And to John, **"Behold your mother!"** [7] And, from that moment on John cared for Your mother. Did he outlive all Your disciples and siblings? No parent wants to outlive their children. It violates the nature of nurture and protection that God created in us. She couldn't save You as a mother would. She didn't stop them by swearing out that You weren't who you claimed. She knew who You were. She didn't have Joseph to turn to for comfort for he was surely dead. But if he had been alive, he would have been silent too, as he knew too that You were the son of God. And this is such an important part of Your crucifixion.

You loved Your mother and even in Your death and return to heaven, You planned for her care until her call to heaven. Moreover, Your mother, like all the rest of us, needed a Savior. Mary gave birth to the Son of God, and You saved her for all Eternity.

Abba, I say with David, "I treasure Your word in my heart, that I may not sin against You." [8] *It is not just head knowledge, but heart knowledge. It is my entire being, my essence. You have removed the sting of death, Jesus. You gave us victory through the plan of salvation and Your obedience to the Father and the plan. And, with Paul I say, "When this perishable (mortal body) will have put on the imperishable (glorified body), and this mortal will have put on immortality, then will come about the saying that is written,* **"DEATH IS SWALLOWED UP IN VICTORY. O DEATH, WHERE IS YOUR VICTORY? O DEATH WHERE IS YOUR STING?"** [9] *Thank you, Jesus. Amen*

Easter 2013

Bruised, Bloodied, But Not Broken

April 16, 2014 – Abba, it happened again. I let fear get ahead of my faith. I let a medical professional's statement pierce my heart like a cold icy dart. Not once but twice, first an intern then the clinical medicine lead very sincerely pronounced that John had less than six months to live. It was easier to push the words of the intern away, being sick with flu myself; seeing how very sick John had become with it; and hearing other things, the second pronouncement from the kindly doctor with excellent bedside manners made me bleed.

"Why Father? I know better."

I called our daughter, Tammy, as soon as I could. I avoided repeating the whispered words out loud to John when he asked. She said what I knew in my heart. Man, especially ones in white coats, can predict but God is the one who has numbered the hairs on our heads. Of course, their well-intended words might be the reality check I needed, but I doubt that anyone needs to be reminded that their loved one is dying. John wasn't supposed to outlast the life-threatening fungus infection from December, and hospice for two weeks at the end of March wasn't a retreat, so six months from a white coat is almost a promise of life.

But it took me down for a while and still troubles me. I see how difficult living is for him, but I also see a vision of him being well and walking happily through the lobby of our church.

"Are my prayers for his recovery selfish?"

For You, Father, his recovery here is doable. I cannot doubt this. But medicine only sees their inability. This is not difficult for You, but is it Your will? Forgive me for letting fear choke me again; for taking my eyes off You and looking at the water, looking at the storm around us; strengthen my faith and let me be here for John as he needs; and give me the wisdom I need for this. John is Yours. Heal him, LORD.

We walk by Faith and not Fear – not today or ever.

Jesus, we celebrate Your sacrificial death and glorious resurrection this Easter season. You are Big Enough. I kneel now at the base of Your cross. I am horrified and physically ill by the cruelty You've suffered, and I look away. I hear You speak into the swirling oppressive darkness,

"My God, my God, why have You forsaken me?" [1]

You look at me steadfastly peering into my soul. I know then that the suffering and the cross was all for me. My spirit cries within me for I cannot speak. "My God, my God forgive me." Then, I heard a sigh of satisfaction and the words,

"It is finished. Father, into Your hands I commend My spirit." [2]

Done. Done for me. Father, for we place ourselves into Your hands. To God be all Glory!

April 18, 2014 - Good Friday, Sweet Jesus. It wasn't good for You but became eternal life for us with You. You left the Eternal throne room of God the Father and squeezed Your Glorified being into a tiny human infant. You joined an earthly family for thirty years before starting Your ministry amongst us. You drew twelve special men to Your side knowing that Satan would take the one who would betray You.

In Your own humanity, You became comfortable with the humanity You created at a level not held since the Garden. You knelt in Gethsemane to pray that the plan of salvation might be modified to spare You the ordeal of the Cross. Your unparalleled anguish then was evident in great drops of bloody sweat. In Your human form, the Beloved Only Son, You were waiting for the answer from the Holy Father. The answer still is heard!

The Father said, **"No"**. God said **"No"** to You the Beloved, so that we, the created, might have a means of escape.

You replied, "Not my will, but Yours." [3]

And the events that started there in the Garden of Gethsemane with Your acceptance of the Father's holy will has not ended yet. For each time a new believer prays for salvation, the legacy of the "No" to Your answered prayer saves another created soul for all eternity. God said, "No" to You to say "Yes" to anyone who asks for forgiveness. You laid down Your life and took it up again for me; and all the souls who asked and all the souls who will ask, until God says, **"Son, go gather the children."**

Good Friday was exceptionally good for me, Holy Trinity, for the plan of my restoration to you was not only complete but I gained Your Holy Spirit to live within me as my source and guide to my eternal home. Thank you, Jesus, for taking on human flesh, humanity's sin, and gaining victory over Death. Thank you for my life and the life of all You have called Your Own. Your death and resurrection, Your great suffering, not only saves, but brings the comfort of knowing that You, the One, who suffered torture, humiliation, and death for me, now stands as my advocate beside the Father's throne. You are John's advocate with God. You gave Your all for me then, and now advocate at God's throne all that is right and good for me. **You have not forgotten John.**

You know that human life isn't easy, but the plan didn't pay for easy but simple.
Asking for forgiveness and receiving the gift of salvation,
Already paid, is simple for any who would ask.
Living this life isn't easy in the flesh but living it with Your advocacy is simple.
We face each day in Your unconditional love.
Eternity where the immortal soul puts on the immortal glorified body is simple,
Because like salvation it is not done in our human power.
It is done by Your great power and love.

I catch glimpses of Glory now and then.
Jesus, I look forward to having You who loved me so much,
And who loves me even still, love me in the presence of the Father,
And all the gathered saints in my glorified immortal body.
Do I not have more loved ones there than here?
All praise, honor, and glory, now and forever. Amen.

Easter 2014

Abba, when I wrote this John was still with us and we did not know how soon You were planning on receiving him forever home. You answered one last prayer for us when John went home(May 9, 2014) for I was with him when he died and more, I saw his spirit leave. I did not see it leave any of the other four I was privileged to be with when they went home. Thank you. I do believe in the eternal and peace for those You call to the Eternal. Your world without end, forever and always. Love your daughter, Rhoda. Amen.

Eternal Beings

Abba, You created Adam and Eve as eternal beings forming them with
Your own hands and making them living spirits with Your own breath.
They were made by You in the image of the Trinity and lived with daily visits from
You in the Garden of Eden.
Then Satan, the father of lies and a murderer, deceived them.
And their sin of disobedience set them and us on a path to death.

They were cast from Eden because they could no longer eat from the
Tree of Life and live forever in bodies corrupted by sin.
Outside the garden their physical bodies declined.
In time, they returned to the dust of the earth.
But You in Your mercy could not allow their eternal souls to live forever in sin.
So, Christ came to be the payment for our restoration to You.

You made Adam and Eve and us eternal beings.
From the time their hearts and our hearts first started to beat we are alive.
But physical death happens, death over which Christ gained victory.
Death a defeated enemy cannot be victorious over the righteous.
"God has made everything beautiful in its time.
He has also set eternity in our hearts,
yet we cannot understand God." [1]

You did not create us to experience death.
With the knowledge of eternity in our hearts we struggle against death.
For we were created to live forever in harmony with You.
But eternal life in harmony with You was lost in the garden—oh not!
But since You made us eternal beings You provide us with
Gloried, eternal bodies when our fragile earth suits fail.
So, our mortal bodies perish and we take our immortal bodies.

Abba wants you to get a little excited! Our eternal souls and spirits don't die.
They are joined with *immortal* bodies that will live forever with the Trinity .
When a caterpillar spins a cocoon in its life cycle
And then struggles to emerge a butterfly—
No one exclaims over the loss of the caterpillar.
We watch in pleasure as the butterfly gains its wings and flies!

The butterfly lacks the free will God created in us.
It cannot choose where it will live the days of its life.
We have the freewill to choose to live through Christ <u>with</u> God.
For we are eternal beings who will live forever in heaven or hell.
Hell, the place of eternal separation (death) away from God.

Hell is the only place of true death.
There in eternal agony the deceived cannot find rest or satisfaction.
They have no second chance to be redeemed by the blood of Christ.
They get no do overs.

Abba, I have attended the deaths of many family members. Each who were saved died in Christ to resurrected bodies and were given robes of righteousness to clothe their gloried immortal bodies. I attended their deaths and funerals, but they are very much alive, and they are very excited to be living with Christ knowing that I will someday join them.

Abba, John's journey into death was not quick like my maternal grandmother's death. She died within a few hours of her last stroke. John's death from a form of leukemia took years. When John's health first declined, we passed it off as aging and family genetics.

What we denied was the possibility of John's Vietnam service causing problems four decades later, but denial didn't alter the course of his disease. December 2006 in hindsight was a red flare, but we didn't push for answers until March 2010. Our first hematology facility couldn't find an answer. So, we gratefully remained in our cocoon of ignorance. But by January 2011, Abba, we knew Primary Myelofibrosis, which we couldn't even pronounce let alone understand.

John became transfusion dependent on January 13, 2012, receiving more than 350 units of red blood cells and plateletpheresis through May 2014. Born in 1950, he was a good son, brother, husband, father, uncle — a good man who went to church with me and our children but was not saved until October 1985.

Abba, John never complained and if he did, I never heard it. His course of treatment outside the transfusions included medication, chemotherapy, a failed stem-cell transplant at the Mayo Clinic in Scottsdale Arizona, and ten surgeries for compartment syndrome and a mucor sinus fungal infection that was neither diagnosed nor treated promptly. We believed in his recovery even after the failed transplant and "always fatal" fungal infection.

And John fully recovered from the fungal infection, and the loss of the infected tissue in his lower right arm and skin graft. He didn't die from the failed stem cell transplant. He died when he had nothing left and his cancer turned to Acute Myelogenous Leukemia. Even then he wanted to protect me and needed me to say, "I'd be ok."

Abba, we never asked why this happened. It happened because he was exposed to chemicals of warfare in Vietnam. We didn't ask why You allowed it. We know the consequences of freewill led to his death. John chose the Army and volunteered for Vietnam when he was young and invincible, and men in government and business were out to make profits, if not win a war.

I still don't ask why You didn't grant him an extraordinary miracle of healing, because You did, it just wasn't in his mortal body. Abba, I still wonder why he had to go through all that he went through? What I can write in a summary doesn't describe the anguish and agony of his illness, complications, ten surgeries, transfusions, transplant, and hospital days. I remember what my love of forty-three years suffered clearly. I was with him up to twenty-four hours a day.

I know he treasured his days with us and us with him. Which day would I give up now? One of the blessings of being away for five months in our Arizona sojourn was we were just us two again with You. All I can imagine in answer is that the scope of his suffering has to do with the amount of his reward in heaven.

John's last question May 7, 2014, at 5:30 am, "Why can't I just die?" You answered, May 9, 2014, at 12:30 pm when You received him home. I was privileged to be with him and watch his spirit depart his body. Eternity beckoned, and John gratefully left behind what he no longer needed for what waited. The moment he left he was no longer ill or sixty-four.

Abba, I have our journal from our Arizona days and John's last four months at home. You know Tammy posted an entry each day to Facebook to Mustard Seed Faith. A few people followed John's journey. For me living those days just wasn't the adage one day at a time, but the reality of not anticipating or trying to live any future day. It was living with Your Presence being very real. John wasn't much of a talker, but when he said something it was important.

Abba, John saw in his recovery as an opportunity to tell disabled and struggling veterans that You were very real and very much still a God of miracles. In his last days when he still had the energy he prayed aloud twice. I no longer remember the words, but still feel the quiet beauty of the words a man of few words spoke aloud to You and shared with me and a chaplain.

He dreamed of himself dancing with a granddaughter at her wedding. He saw unfinished future days, but we did get our extraordinary miracle. And, perhaps he is sharing stories now with veterans and them with him as he waits to dance with all of his granddaughters. He was the one who got to hold the unborn grandchild last year that left us before he or she knew this life.

Abba, I don't have all the answers, but I don't have to because I know the One who does. And I know that none of my questions will be asked once I get to heaven because there the things of earth will have no power over us.

John's earthly tent collapsed and from the wreckage he escaped the boundaries of disease, medicine, and time and he waits for me. Someday I too will step away from my fragile earth suit and be escorted by an angel or two to Your throne room. Then in my white robe of righteousness I will kneel at my Savior's feet and be welcomed to heaven and all those in eternity will greet me with joy, more joy than the grief of those I leave behind.

The only downside to death I see is for those who don't know or trust You. For those of us who know You, it is the loss of time with those we love as we remain here without them. It is not sharing with those who have gone ahead the events we have left. Grief isn't permanent but a period where our tears are collected by You, and we receive Your comfort. You are in all our days, if we remain open and allow Your presence to surround us and fill us. We can live here because You, The Trinity do.

You are the Creator of all our days, and You will finish the temporary phase here and give us eternal days where there is no calendar or clock. Amen.

Legacy

There is a legacy of darkness, pain, suffering, and death passed down to each newborn.
They are born into a world deprived of its true nature and beauty.
The world they're given has polluted waterways, and mountains built of waste and decay.
Their lives are counted as without value under the government of self-willed greedy men.
They hear voices spew half-truths and lies, perhaps sincere, believed, but taught as truth.

Who will save the earth, the children, the helpless infants, the old?
Who will come to rescue them from medicine, empty foods, and electronic play?
Who will prevent their enslavement from vile drugs and death laced vices?
Who can overcome the plots of men who plunder their lives for evil profit and pleasure?
Who can save this humanity who seek something better than mere survival?

What can they do? To whom can they turn?
Who will tell them the truth? Who will wipe away their tears?
Terrors plague them day and night.
Who will banish this evil and their fears?
Who will pierce the darkness and be their light?

Wait, I see a distant light.
Yes, from its strong glow, the darkness tries to hide.
Still down through the centuries it shines.
A Holy Light, God's only Son from Bethlehem emerged.
This divine light came to save man and was not extinguished on Golgotha's hill.

Surely man in his ignorance led by evil's own hand caused Him pain.
He, the Lamb of God, was subject to the suffering due them.
But they pierced Him for their transgressions.
Cursed, bruised, bloodied, and tortured Him for their iniquities.
They punished Him and He brought them peace and His wounds offered healing to them.

Christ's life was poured out an offering for man's sin.
Yet, there was no violence in Him, and He was silent before them.
He was numbered among the transgressors and bore their sins.
He was crucified between two convicts and placed in a borrowed tomb.
The temple priest and Roman government sealed and guarded His place of rest.

There He set the captives free and obtained the keys to hell and death.
He died in human flesh to ransom His creation and to give them life.
He is alive evermore, raised from the tomb and at the right hand of the God.
Why did Christ pay the price to ransom man?
God through His own Son gave man this victory over sin and death.

The cost was paid by <u>love,</u> and Jesus' own willing sacrifice.
Oh, let the price be applied to you.
Oh, sinful men take up your cross and follow Him!
What is the cost to follow Jesus?
He went silently to death and to the tomb.
But beloved while His wounded body rested, He went boldly into hell.

What is the cost to you?
It is but your life, but it will not be lost but saved.
In Christ Jesus, all who trust and believe walk in the newness of life.
All the paltry things the earth has to offer them have grown wearisome and dim.
They want nothing less for they are only satisfied in Jesus Christ.

They once were lost. It was their legacy.
Their lives bore the crimson stain of trespass and sin.
But, they asked, and their sin was cleansed and washed away by His blood.
Jesus' cruel crucifixion, death, and resurrection then applied to them.
They are now dead to sin and alive forevermore with Him.

Are you lost in your trespasses with eternal death your destiny?
Surely you must want to be set free.
Reach out your hand in supplication and take your rescuer's hand.
Jesus will pull you into His loving arms and apply His death to your penalty.
Yes, live in Him debt free, but more live in Him eternally.

Do not be deceived, beloved.
You were not born to live briefly only then to die.
Your earthly body is subject to disease and death.
But you are more than flesh and bone.
There is a soul, a spirit inside of you that will live on.

Your soul, eternal living spirit, will one day move to the eternal plane.
But it is here on earth you must choose your destiny.
Will you live in a body glorified in Paradise, or suffer the eternal agony called hell?
Both destinations are real for death and the grave is not final.
Choose to live in Christ and let His love be your legacy.

Easter March 16, 2016

Father, thank you for meeting with me. I can think of no greater legacy I can leave but my faith. I do believe, Father, I truly believe and want my legacy for my children, grandchildren, and all that are here with me now or who will speak about me when I am at last home, to speak of me and my unshakable faith in You. It was passed down to me, Father and I cherish it. Let all those who bear my DNA or even know me, share my legacy of faith. This is the dynasty I want to continue. Most gracious and Holy Father, Amen.

My Heart

My heart is filled to overflowing with joy
And it rightfully sings an anthem of praise
That words alone cannot relieve.

My heart sees only glimpses of the universe
You called into existence and cannot
Comprehend its depth or beauty.

My heart is at a lost to explain its awe
Over a single leaf and cannot breathe for the magnitude
Of the beauty of this created sphere.

My heart rejoices that You have called me
Your beloved Daughter and the price
Of my relationship was paid by another.

My heart marvels at Your Son, my Beloved Savior
Who I call Redeemer and Advocate as He
Paid the whole cost of my restoration once and forever for me.

My heart gladdens to see the Light for
I know it casts out darkness and fear and
Truth is revealed as all shadows must slink away.

My heart glows when it sees new life and beholds
Its potential to fulfill the plan You have
Created for that dear little one.

My heart understands that You have a divine
Plan for my life and strives to obey the
Guideposts laid out along the path before me.

My heart takes comfort in knowing that You
Are my Advocate, Counselor, and Healer,
And that Your death has gained victory over death for me.

My heart acknowledges sadness for grief has come to visit
But grief cannot linger but a little while for death
Has lost its sting and been swallowed up in sweet victory.

My heart finds peace in knowing that
You are in every storm, every valley, every tragedy
That befalls me, and You can redeem it for good.

My heart bursts with the gladness and joy
Of being wholly and rightfully Yours, Holy Father
And the spirit living inside of me tingles.

My heart is dancing in the vision of that
Great day when the darkness will be cast down into
The eternal abyss of damnation and we will see only the Light.

My spirit sings our private anthem of love and praise
In anticipation of being in Your presence forever
For it was redeemed by Christ's sacrifice.

Your servant's heart is made so joyful in You, O LORD,
And wants to finish its days in You as You
Meet the needs of all Your children.

Easter 2016

Dear Father, it is my first Easter without Mom, even if she couldn't be with me in church, I would have shared part of the day with her. She used to proofread the pieces given to me. Now this is something she won't see, but Father, please accept it as praise from my heart. I know without You this wouldn't exist for You are my source and the Your Spirit speaks these words to me. I have seen a lot of death in my life, but I am ever grateful that You abide in my heart, so it is not swallowed up by grief, but basks in the glow of Your love and sweet comfort. Yet, a little while, I wait patiently because I wait in You. My heart sings the song of Eternity. All Praise, Father, Son, and Holy Spirit. Amen!

Redemption's Glorious Plan

The palm branches are dry and brittle and have been trampled into the ground
By cart wheels, Roman horses, burdened donkeys,
And hundreds of feet scurrying about in their ordinary lives.
For those who watched or participated in that First Palm Sunday, the triumphant
Entry of Christ into Jerusalem became a shadowed memory as more was yet to come.
But many would not see or understand God's holy plan fulfilled.
The people had a momentary escape from their dull, harsh lives, but the deeper meaning,
Their adoration of the true King's arrival in Jerusalem was lost to them.
Judas you were there with Christ, the Lamb of God,
Along with His other disciples and followers.
How did you miss what the prophet said?
How was Zechariah's prophecy beyond any to grasp?

Rejoice greatly, Daughter Zion! Shout, Daughter Jerusalem!
See, your King comes to you, righteous and victorious,
lowly and riding on a donkey on a colt, the foal of a donkey.[1]

Oh, the people gathering for Passover rejoiced, but the self-righteous religious leaders
Shook in anger, and plotted to separate Christ from the adoring crowds, and then kill Him.
Oh Judas, how could you have allowed yourself to be the pawn of the enemy
And to betray God's only Son, who came to rescue you?
You were a part of His inner circle. You saw Him feed the many with so little food;
Food dealt out by your own hand.
You saw Him heal the sick, cast out demons, restore eyesight, make broken
Bodies whole and bring the dead to life. You even did this in His power when He sent you out.
Yet, you, Judas were somehow dead to His holy presence.
Oh, how could you not have felt or understood His love, His compassion, or His divinity?
Oh, wayward man, how could you have been privy to His parables disclosed,
And still negotiate a bounty for His precious head?
Oh, do not point an accusing finger at me for I know I am no better than you!

You ate one last Passover meal with Him and the other disciples.
How did you feel when Jesus humbled Himself and knelt to wash your feet?
Yet, that night the scriptures were fulfilled for you shared His bread
And turned against Him. Your purse was enriched with the silver of the price of a lowly slave,
Which the priest gladly paid, but, let me momentarily ponder this.
Would you have betrayed Christ for a few coins if Satan himself hadn't entered you?
You left the Passover celebration all too soon, and how much you did miss.
Jesus prayed for me that night and for all those who would receive the message of salvation.

You were not present in the garden when He prayed in agony to the Father,
For He knew the agony of the separation from His Father the coming hours would bring.
"My soul is overwhelmed with sorrow to the point of death. Stay here and keep watch with Me."
He prayed the bitter cup He was about to drink could otherwise be satisfied.
So great then was His anguish, His sweat became like great drops of blood falling to the ground.
"My Father, if it is possible, may this cup be taken from Me. Yet not as I will, but as You will." [2]
Then, an angel came from heaven to comfort and to strengthen Him.
Yes, the great struggle of our very human Savior and the divine Son of God
Who came to save us was won by His sovereign love for all mankind.

But you, Judas, betrayer of the Lamb, with Satan in control of you,
Led a mob headed by Roman soldiers to Christ's frequent place of prayer,
And there you betrayed Him with your unholy lips with a customary kiss.
That night was not overcome by torch light for the darkness in you was too great.
But even still when my Beloved LORD identified Himself to the Roman centurion,
"I am He."

You, and all gathered there to arrest Him, fell <u>back</u> and down to the ground.
Even you, with the enemy inside of you, could not stand
And so, had to bow at our dear Savior's feet.
Did your soul not *writhe* then to be free of your dark master?
Did you struggle to your feet, and want to take a sword with Peter and defend
The One you had so recently called LORD?
Did you marvel briefly at Christ's control?
He did not call angels to His side but restored Malchus' ear with His healing touch.
And protected those who stood with Him, and commanded dear Peter,
"Put your sword away! Shall I not drink the cup the Father has given Me?" [3]

When He was led away and the disciples fled in fear,
Did you too try to run from your awful deed and the darkness frothing inside of you?
Or did you follow to watch your loathsome deed unfold?
Surely Satan would have enjoyed watching Christ's cruel handling.
When you knew Christ was condemned to die, were you last free of the enemy?
For, too late then you tried to return the silver coins.

With Satan no longer with you the shame was all on you to bear.
Like me, you could not take back the sting of what your choice had wrought.
Was there any satisfaction for you when you tossed the coins into the temple?
How could there be?
You judged yourself guilty, condemned yourself to die
And hung your sorrowing self upon a tree. Then, your bloated corpse
Left alone, perhaps for days, fell free and burst upon the ground.
You were buried in that very field, called even now the field of blood,
because in your name with your betraying coins the unholy priest did buy it.
At judgment time, will these priests fare any better than you?
You did go back to them in remorse for the innocent blood you betrayed, but
Were they ever more than glad? Will this be held in your favor at God's judgment seat?

Did you, Judas, a man once identify with Christ, see Christ's agony as
He was crucified for me on the old-rugged cross between two thieves?
I believe not. Christ went to Golgotha's Hill, and you surely went the other way.
You surely would not have wanted to be seen by the few who stood by Him.
Even with a truly sorrowful heart, you could have not faced Mary and choked out the words,
"I am so sorry. I didn't mean for it to come to this."
Judas, you couldn't know that He refused the bitter wine mixed with gall to relieve His suffering,
He wanted to remain clear, suffering fully in my stead, and so was alert and prepared to offer comfort.
No, you never saw Christ's agony on the cross, or heard Christ's conversation with the confessing thief,
"Jesus, remember me when You come into Your kingdom."
You, because of your greedy deed, could not benefit from it as did the thief.
Jesus answered him, "Truly I tell you, today you will be with Me in paradise."

One dying thief that day lost his life upon his worthy cross and so writhes in eternal death.
But the other thief found his relief in my Redeemer and gained eternal life through Him.
Oh, Judas, I would that you could gain eternal life through the One who died for all mankind.
But you in life chose to follow the path of those who scorn the Lamb.
God the Father, who loved the Son, abandoned Him that day because God in His Holiness
Could not look on sin and Christ became the sin of the world that day!
God shrouded the whole of the land in darkness while Christ hung on the cross for me.
His divine nature withstood the torture of the cross longer than a human body should,
And yet His separation from God weighed on Him even more.
From His tortured body, mind, and burdened spirit He called out.
"My God, my God, why hast thou forsaken me?" [5]
He could not call Him Father for He had not the right, dying as man for all mankind.

His innocent blood poured out that day like no other. No, He didn't deserve to die!
The care of His mother watching at His feet, He did give to John the Beloved disciple.
He even gave up His earthly family and friends for the likes of you and me!
When Jesus hung upon the cross I deserved said,
"I am thirsty."
He spoke of His desire for the souls of men for which He willingly suffered and died.
Then, and only then when my dear LORD had finished all He came to do and scripture was fulfilled,
He gave up His life for no soldier, priest, not even the enemy could take it from Him.
He said, *"Father! Into Your hands I commit My spirit."*
He then released His spirit long trapped in an earthly shell with these last words.
"Tetelestai" "It is finished." [6]

Yes, the price of sin was paid once for all at Calvary that day for all who would believe.
Christ, the Lamb of God, was the perfect chosen sacrifice indeed.
To my debt of sin His death has been applied. And my name is now recorded
In the Book of Life, and "Paid in Full" in His precious blood is stamped beside it.
Now, Christ did not idly rest in His borrowed tomb,
He went to hell and set the captives free and took away with Him the keys to hell and death.
Yes, He gained victory for me over sin, hell, and death.
He, like the captives, freed me to live in Him.
And, when at last, He frees my spirit and my soul from its earthly dwelling,
I will live forever there in Paradise and meet the eternal living man, once called thief.

Oh, wretched Judas, you had the same opportunity to gain heaven
And you tossed it away like those thirty silver coins.
Christ would not have withheld salvation from you.
You, like every other man, had to choose that Christ's promises weren't meant for you.
Hell was not created for man, not even you,
But for the angels who despised their role.
For those angels who followed Satan from heaven,
No longing serving their Creator's plans,
But their fallen master's treacherous schemes,
Seeking souls to burn forever in the fires meant just for them.

Look at Judas and flee his dark path the enemy would have you choose.
Dearest family and friends look to the light shining from Golgotha's Hill.
Christ was the only sacrifice that was good enough to save men's souls.
Resurrection Sunday came and the heavy stone, by angels, was removed,
And the Roman stamp that sealed the tomb,
Nor the Roman guards on duty there could stop the Son.
Christ took up His scarred body, leaving the unneeded grave linens behind
For He was alive when He rose from the empty tomb.
His disciples all saw Him, but sadly Judas you could not.
Even now Christ is His beloved children's advocate in heavenly places.
Choose Him, beloved, the One who paid your debt and follow
His lighted path that will lead you safely home to eternity with Him.

March 25, 2016

I had not thought of writing today, Father. I thought You gave me my Good Friday writing already, but to my great joy, You gave me this. Tetelestai was Christ's statement that not only means. "It is finished" but an accounting phase that means, "paid in full." Thank you, thank you for all the Trinity has done and will yet do! Eternal praise be raised, heard, and accepted. Holy Father, Creator, Son, and Holy Spirit, again thank you. Amen!

Peace Be With You

A sheep's contentment lies in recognizing His Shepherd's voice.
Jesus is the Chief Good Shepherd.
Our Good Shepherd who laid down His life for us.
He paid the cost of our salvation and restoration.

He withstood false imprisonment and trial.
He shrouded His perfection with all our sins.
He endured merciless beatings and death for our crimes.

But our great Good Shepherd did not leave us.
Even in death He provided for our future.
In His death He overcame hell and death.

He set the captives free.
Victoriously He gained the keys of hell and death.
He opened the gates to eternal life for each of His beloved.

Precious Jesus, our Good Shepherd was resurrected and returned to heaven.
There He advocates for us with Our Father.
Who better to advocate for us than Jesus who died for us?

Triune love created us and will not suffer our loss.
Father and Son direct angels to attend us.
The Holy Spirit lives in us as our constant source and guide.

Obedience is the key to our fellowship and peace.
Prayer is our key to unlock the resources of heaven.
Grace and mercy come new each day from the mercy tree.

The Chief Shepherd shows us favor. Our Good Shepherd
Gives us courage, strength, peace, faith, and hope.
He has plans to give us a future here and eternity with Him.

Learn His voice in the quiet times, so you can hear it in the storms.
Step out of the boat and walk over troubled waters.
He will hold you up as He is right beside you.

Don't look at the dark clouds, wind, rain, or waves.
Keep your eyes focused on the Good Shepherd.
He has a good plan for each of us while we live on this unrestored earth.
Keep your eyes on Jesus, the eternal prize.

The Good Shepherd will lead you to green pastures and still waters,
Through shadowed valleys and the silent abode safely home.

Easter April 16, 2017

The Betrothal
(Jesus and the Church)

The Groom speaks tenderly to His Bride,
*"I loved you before the foundations of the world were set
And created the universe for your home.
Our desire to share all with you was so great that My Father spoke, and the expanse obeyed.
Yet, its vastness, complexity, and beauty were not nearly
Enough for you needed a special home.
So, the Milky Way was strewn and your planet a speck of dust came forth.
It was set into delicate motion to orb safely with its moon and sun amongst the stars.
A barren forbidding earth would not do but required
So much beauty as to take your breath away.
There a garden beautiful teaming with life was planted and grew.
Yes, my beloved, Eden was created for your first parents, and We loved them as we do you."* [1]

The bride then answers her Beloved Groom,
"How could you love me so deeply before I even came to be?
It is too much for me to understand the Love that created the universe.
I have not seen all the earth does offer but understand that men still explore and marvel at it.
How deep is the ocean and high the mountains here yet even they cannot touch the sky?
Plant and animal life for food and beauty and yet not all found and categorized.
Jungles and deserts, the bitter arctic too, such variety is too much for me.
How do I understand the Knowledge and Love that created such a home for me?"

The Groom responds to His beloved,
*"How could We not want to share with you all that delighted Us?
When the evil one came and destroyed the Perfection We did not falter in Our Love.
We then implemented Our plan of salvation to restore you, Our beloved.
So, I came for you in human form and gave My life, the full price of reparation.
Yet, I did not subjugate you to My will, but allowed you to choose Me on your own.
What joy heaven shared when you came to Me and allowed Me to make you My own.
Only then, was I able to cherish you, lavishing you with My love and care.
Then the Holy Spirit Sweet came to you, so you'd never have to sojourn on your own again."* [2]

The bride responds in glad adoration to her Beloved Groom.
"I remember the joy of our betrothal day Beloved.
The love of the Trinity flooded my heart, mind, spirit, and soul in an instant.
My thirst for what I had been created for at last replete.
I abandoned the world forsaking all others for You.
I sought Your heart and Yours alone, although I did disappoint at times.
Our desire for You and all things eternal from that day grew.
Even in life's darkest moments we found comfort in Your love.
We learned to look for joy in every day and never found it lacking."

The Groom encourages His Beloved with promises of the future.
"I was never idle in My love for you; for I cherish you, forgive you, and My love is ever true.
Knowing when your mortal days would end, I prepared a new dwelling for your soul.
So, once you shed your earthly tent you will put on your new home eternal in the heavens.
Then, and only then beloved, will you see all I have prepared for you.
'Eye has not seen, nor ear heard, and you cannot imagine what awaits you there.'
So, let me paint a picture of your eternal home." [3]

"The Holy Eternal City, the new Jerusalem, is set high on a hill
And shines with the Shekinah glory of Father God.
My Father is its only light, and I am its lamp.
There is no night, but only the day for His brilliance is like a jewel.
Your new uncrowded home is fourteen-hundred miles in length, in breath, and height.
Its walls are two-hundred feet thick and are made of jasper, pure gold, as pure as glass.
The wall has twelve foundations bearing the names of my twelve apostles.
The city street on which your feet will trod is made of fine gold as clear as glass."

"The city walls are adorned with every kind of jewel:
Emerald, onyx, amethyst, topaz and more.
The colors of heaven will burst upon you true unlike your old home and what you knew.
This great city made for you has twelve gates each made from a single pearl.
Three gates on each side with angels assigned to watch each gate.
The gates are never shut, and each bears the name of a tribe of Israel.
Through these gates, you, My beloved, will travel in and out of the city."

"A river, clear as crystal, flows from Our Thrones down beside the main street.
On each side of the river there is a tree of life.
Each tree of life yields twelve kinds of fruit – a fresh crop every month.
The leaves of the tree of life will be for your healing.
There will be no temple for worship as We will live amongst you there.
And you beloved will reign with us forever and ever.
In your eternal form your life will know no end." [4]

The bride responds, her fervor rising,
"Beloved, our souls were made to share Your eternal love.
How long must I wait for our wedding day?
The vision of heaven beautiful You paint pales as we think of seeing You.
Even now we watch as the heavenly choir's crescendo ends
And angels watch for our approach.
We see Your loving eyes and Your smile encourages us to take our place beside You.
How far away the things of earth, the injustices, the sorrows, and regrets seem now.
All our questions fade and dissipate as Your assurance fills each of us."

The Beloved Groom asks,

"Wait patiently for just a little longer, beloved, that Eternal day will come.
Rest in Me for you cannot be taken from My Father's hand. [5]
You are Mine beloved, and I am yours, yet Our plans for you are not now complete.
How beautiful you are to Me, and My desire is for you to be with Me.
I have put a seal over your heart knowing it beats for me and eternity.
The Father knows you are all I ever wanted. Learn more of Me while you wait.
The time will come, and I will reach out for you and say,
"Hurry beloved. This is the day."
You'll come in fervent anticipation and say, "Your bride is ready, joyful for Eternal day." [6]

February 14, 2018

Dear Father, the date on this piece is right. It is a wonderful Valentine gift more so because Easter on April 1, this year is, John's, my beloved valentine's birthday. It was inspired by something I heard in our Bible study and the scriptures come from Revelation and John the disciple's vision of heaven. You know all the hard work by this Bible study author and Your Bible study teacher is all worth it. I get spiritually fed in class and my Bible study classmates add to my learning experience. Thank you, for the authors, the teachers, and the other students. They all provide much needed spiritual nourishment for me. Forever and ever, LORD, Your world without end. Amen!

Road to Emmaus [1]
The Lessor Chosen

Step through time and walk the narrow road with two,
travel between Jerusalem and Emmaus just seven miles for you.
Two disciples are walking there, not one of the eleven chosen,
But two of the seventy sent out in pairs by Jesus.
Sent out to prepare His way to preach in Judea. [2]

You will be walking with Cleopas, Joseph's brother, who was married to a Mary.
He was Jesus' step uncle and his sons also served in Jesus' ministry.
Now the other there with you may be Luke for he authored the story,
Not identifying himself as was the custom of the day or you may be
with Mary traveling home with her husband. Who is a bit of a mystery?

This Mary stood with Mary, Jesus' mother, Mary Magdalene,
And several women at Christ's cross.
She saw with the other women the atrocities and painful death of one she held dear.
She was well aware of the empty tomb, the forsaken shroud and folded face cloth.
She witnessed an angel tell them that Christ was not there but alive!
She ran from the tomb in joy to tell the others who were in hiding!

Yet, you know, not just the women but Peter and John testified to seeing the empty tomb.
Mary Magdalene had been first to see the risen LORD. [3] Still they remain hidden behind
Locked doors in Jerusalem, but you are on the road home.
You are going to Emmaus as two discuss what has been seen and reported.
So, you listen as Cleopas and Mary, Mary let's believe, converse and reason over these events.
Then, wait, you are no longer three on the road but four.

The stranger on the road you are not restrained to see, but they do not know Him.
He asks them, **"What things?"** [4] They are discussing things that make them so sad.
You hear them speak of the crucifixion and their hope that Jesus was the One.
They acknowledge to the stranger, to your Jesus, that this is the third day since His crucifixion.
Atlas, they do not understand but your heart wants to shout to them the victory.

Oh but, Jesus, chides them in love and teaches them,
"O foolish ones, <u>and slow of heart</u> to believe
In all that the prophets have spoken!
Ought not the Messiah to have suffered
These things and to enter into His glory?" [5]

Then, our beloved Jesus opens up the scriptures to them concerning Himself.
He starts with Moses and goes through all the Prophets,
Explaining all the Scriptures had to say about His coming and His death! [6]
Perhaps three hours pass as you walk beside them and hear the good news.
And you delight in this time with the newly risen LORD with these lessor two
Who were among the first to see Jesus alive!

Dusk has fallen and it is dinner time as they arrive home and Jesus was going on further.
They restrained him with a plea. "Turn aside and abide with us."
Jesus enters with them to sup.
The table set, He took the bread and blessed and broke it, and gave some to each.
"Then their eyes were opened, and they knew Him; and He vanished from their sight. [7]
"Yes." You shout and pump your arm in victory. They understand a little more.

You watch silently. Stunned, their confusion clears as their astonished hearts ignite.
They had been with the risen LORD, walked the dusty road with Him as He opened the
scriptures to them, shared their home, and He blessed and broke the bread for them.
Finding their voices, you hear them say to one another,
"Did not our heart burn within us while He talked with us?" [8]

The meal and the dangers of the dark road forgotten for their disillusioned hearts
Are on fire again, you race back with them to Jerusalem.
Finding the eleven and those gathered there, they joyously repeat their story. [9]
Finding then too, they Jesus has appeared to Peter and then many others. [10]
The darkness of their despair and their grieving tears now turned to joy.

The hour goes late, and you now must return to your time.
Before you step through the portal home you study each of them.
Thomas you know won't allow himself to believe until he sees Jesus for himself.
Peter will get to make amends for his thrice denial.
Each of them will share the gospel and each will be martyred for their faith.

Does not your heart burn within you for this Jesus?
Does not your passion for Him light up your soul?
Does the Holy Spirit living in you dance with you in joy?
This Jesus, Perfect Sacrifice, Risen Savior, and Advocate loves you.
This Jesus who will be with you at your journey's end at the Father's throne.

Celebrate Jesus! Amen!

For Kay, September 28, 2019

Dear Father, once again when I try to take a scripture story and put it into my own words, to go deeper, I stumble again and again. Jesus revealed Himself to the two on the road to Emmaus who had found enough courage to come out of hiding and travel home to spread the word of Jesus' death. It seems reasonable to me that Jesus would have appeared to His aunt and uncle who had been in His ministry, and whose sons also served Him. Cleopas certainly wouldn't have left his Mary in Jerusalem. This story gives me hope, LORD, that You, the Trinity, love us all the same whether great or small, Jew or Gentile. Thank you, Jesus, for revealing Yourself to a woman first, Mary Magdalene, to Peter, to Your family, to Your followers, and to Thomas just as they each needed. Thank you for revealing Yourself to us. Thank you for Kay's request to write this, because I learned so much, and the Holy Spirit gave this to me. It seems it was meant to be, and I missed the call to write it. Even so, You know before this Bible study that this story resonated with me. I love the humanness, the emotionalism, of these very real people who experienced You and grew as a result, enough to die for You. It gives me hope for myself. I see the continuity between the past, the present, and the future, and know when time is complete the circle will be closed. ∞ Your creation without end, will be restored, forever. ∞ Amen!

Jesus, "I AM"

One of the most powerful moments of Jesus' life was recorded by John. Jesus had eaten the last supper with His disciples; prayed for them and us, prayed in the Garden of Gethsemane while His closest friends slept; and was comforted by an angel who came to strengthen Him. Then, knowing and accepting His fate, Jesus went out to meet His betrayer, Judas, and Judas' master Satan, as well as the soldiers, temple servants, and the mob who came to arrest Him in the darkness away from the adorning populace who sought Him in the light.

> Scripture reveals, "Jesus, knowing all that was going to happen to Him, went out and asked them,
> **"Who is it you want?"**
> "Jesus of Nazareth," they replied.
> **"I am,"** Jesus said. (And Judas the traitor was standing there with them.)
> <u>And they fell back and down</u>, when He said, **"I am."**
> Again, He asked them, **"Who is it you want?"**
> "Jesus of Nazareth," they said.
> Jesus answered, **"I told you that I am. If you are looking for Me, then let these men go."**
> This happened so that the words He had spoken would be fulfilled:
> **"I have not lost one of those you gave Me."**
> Then Simon Peter drew his sword, and struck the high priest's servant, Malchus, cutting off his right ear.
> Jesus commanded Peter, **"Put your sword away! Shall I not drink the cup the Father has given me?"** [1]

Please remember that Jesus could have escaped them without Peter's help, as He had done before. *They wanted to stone Him, but it wasn't His time or means of death, so He passed through the crowd.* [2] But this is our rash Peter. Peter wanted to defend Jesus, who did not need his help. The soldiers, chief priests and elders of the people coming at Jesus with swords and clubs had just physically drawn back and fell to the ground when Jesus only spoke His name. "**I am.**"

> "So, He spoke to Peter. **"Do you think that I cannot appeal to my Father, and He will at once send me more than twelve legions of angels? But how then should the Scriptures be fulfilled, that it must be so?"** At that hour Jesus said to the crowds, **"Have you come out as a robber against Me, with swords and clubs to capture me? Day after day I sat in the temple teaching, and you did not seize Me. But all this has taken place that the Scriptures of the prophets might be fulfilled."** Then all the disciples left him and fled." [3]

The breath of the Spirit had just forced the mob to the ground. Pause for a moment, God is giving the crowd with weapons a God moment, time to reconsider taking His Beloved Son. How did they feel to draw back and fall-down unwittingly and uncontrollably before Jesus? Were they momentarily confused as they struggled back to their feet? Did they hesitate even for a single moment to put their hands on Him? Did they feel guilt at their assignment?

Oh, but they did get up and so God's plan of salvation proceeded. Peter's human rescue was denied, and Jesus did not call for angelic assistance. So, the trial and crucifixion were on, but Satan would not win. Satan could not win, but we would.

We spent a great deal of reflective time on the crucifixion, but these moments touch me dramatically. Jesus had to clear a path for mankind to crucify Him for us. Think about all the obstacles He overcame, including His own humanity.

Novels, movies, and sadly non-fiction accounts often tell about a person being betrayed by a friend, spouse, or another family member, but what betrayal truly compares to what Jesus allowed? Judas was a part of the inner circle, a chosen disciple, yet as soon as Judas took the bread, Satan entered him.

And Jesus said, "What you are about to do, do quickly." [4] Chilling moment this. Was Jesus speaking to Judas, Satan, or both?

In Exodus, God tells Moses His personal divine name, *Ehyeh,* **I AM.** [5] John tells us that at Jesus' arrest that He identifies Himself as God. Further in Romans, Paul quotes Isaiah: [6]

> *""As surely as I live," says the LORD, "every knee will bow before me;*
> *every tongue will acknowledge God.'"*

This incident was not just Isaiah predicting a future heavenly judgment, but this event. Jesus fulfilled every requirement to be our perfect sacrifice and fulfilled every scripture regarding His life, death, burial, and resurrection. Yet sadly people doubt Jesus' word that He is the only way to heaven.

John quotes Jesus saying, *"**I am** the **way, the truth, and the life. No one comes to the Father except through Me."*** He is not <u>a way</u>, as in one of many; He is **the way**, as in the one and only. [7]

Let's look at Jesus, "**I AM**," as a door/gate.

Like the ark in Noah's day which God closed behind Noah and his family. *"**I am** the door; whoever enters through Me will be saved."* [8]

First Passover homes. The sacrificial blood of a lamb was brushed on the door lintels to protect the lives of all those inside, especially the firstborn. *"When the LORD goes through the land to strike down the Egyptians, He will see the blood on the top and sides of the doorframe and will pass over that doorway, and He will not permit the destroyer to enter your houses and strike you down."* [9]

The curtain/door separating the holy of holies from the people in the temple. *"And Jesus cried out again with a loud voice and yielded up His spirit. And behold, the veil of the temple was torn in two from top to bottom; and the earth shook, and the rocks were split. The tombs were opened, and many bodies of the saints who had fallen asleep were raised; and coming out of the tombs after His resurrection they entered the holy city and appeared to many."* [10] <u>The curtain was 60 feet high, more than 7 stories, 30 feet wide, and four inches thick!</u> God supernaturally rented this in two demonstrating that we were no longer separated from Him! Picture a sword bearing angel!

Think on this more – the darkness at mid-day, the shaking earth, and the resurrection of the saints who had fallen asleep. Family and friends were reunited. God resurrected many dead in Him that day, so we know He will do the same for us. What an awesome God we serve!

Gate of the sheepfold. Jesus our Good Shepherd knows His sheep and His sheep know Him. *Therefore, Jesus said again, "Very truly I tell you, **I am** the gate for the sheep. All who have come before Me are thieves and robbers, but the sheep have not listened to them. **I am** the gate; whoever enters through me will be saved. They will come in and go out and find pastures. The thief comes only to steal and kill and destroy; I have come that they may have life and have it to the full. "**I am** the good shepherd. The good shepherd lays down his life for the sheep."* [11]

Whew! Jesus went through more than my mind can process or my heart can understand to be our Savior. Remember He left heaven to be human, and somehow squeezed His divinity into a tiny infant and subjected Himself to a human body, parents, siblings, friends, and in human form took on our ancient enemy, Satan, and won victory over him when tempted and over Satan in His death. He rose again!

Jesus lived in harmony with His betrayer, Judas, for three years and never took away the man's freewill, or in any way forced him to change. Judas, like us, kept his freewill. Jesus washed Judas' feet and ate one final meal with him knowing His betrayal was set, and that He was already sold into death for the price of a slave.

None of the moments were supernatural as Jesus was in human form. The mocking, humiliation, torture, and crucifixion suffered for us makes me blanch at His physical and mental anguish. Jesus didn't deserve any of the human physical suffering He experienced to pay our sin debt. He didn't deserve the weight of mankind's sin placed on His sinless shoulders. Further, keep this in mind, *He didn't deserve the anguish He endured being separated from His Holy Father during this time.*

How could Jesus have subjected Himself to such abuse, torment, and pain for me is beyond my feeble understanding. God's holiness required Jesus' sacrifice and Jesus accepted it all for you and me. We think of the marks left from the crude spikes hammered into His wrists and feet, and often push aside the sword thrust through His side, because He was already dead.

Don't overlook it again, even in death His very human body was abused for us!

Thomas and Jesus didn't overlook it. John shares this moment with us.

Now Thomas (also known as Didymus), one of the Twelve, was not with the disciples when Jesus came. So, the other disciples told him, "We have seen the LORD!"

But he said to them, "Unless I see the nail marks in his hands and put my finger where the nails were, and put my hand into his side, I will not believe." A week later his disciples were in the house again, and Thomas was with them.

*Though the doors were locked, **Jesus** came and stood among them and said, **"Peace be with you!"** Then he said **to** Thomas, **"Put your finger here; see my hands. Reach out your hand and put it into my side. Stop doubting and believe."***

***Thomas** said to him, "My LORD and my God!"*

*Then Jesus told him, **"Because you have seen me, you have believed; blessed are those who have not seen and yet have believed."** [12]*

Look closely at this because Thomas' doubt ended in his belief and was a gift to us. Jesus bless those of us who weren't born yet, who hadn't seen or known Him in His human form but would believe in our time. Fortunately, Thomas' doubt turned to faith and according to non-biblical references Thomas took the gospel to Parthia, Persia, and India, suffering martyrdom near Madras, at Mt. St. Thomas, India.

In death Jesus wasn't idle, He saw the thief who confessed to Him while they were being crucified to heaven, gained the keys over death and the grave and set the captives free. Feel <u>the tingle</u> in your soul? Then, Jesus was resurrected from His borrowed tomb. Imagine His grave clothes laying relatively undisturbed on the rock slab cut into the hollowed-out tomb. Jesus unlike Lazarus wasn't freed from His shroud, He rose through it, but the Bible tells us His face cloth was left folded neatly. In Jesus' time, when a master crumbled up his dinner napkin it was a sign he was finished and not returning, but if he folded it neatly and laid it beside his plate, he was returning. Jesus' face cloth was neatly folded and laid nearby. This, like the rending of the temple curtain was a symbolic gesture by Jesus. **Jesus is coming back!**

Happy Resurrection Sunday!
March 9, 2018

His Words

His words come down from the cross.
They come to me across the centuries.
Immediately the image on Golgotha's hill comes to mind.
The image of three crosses with three condemned men dying there.
Darkness and death permeate the place and evil gloats over a victory not yet achieved.

His words now echo from His cross centered amongst the three.
He is taunted by the merciless crowd, the Roman centurions, and the thieves dying at His side.
He speaks to the Father including me. *"Father, forgive them, for they know not what they do."* [1]
One thief ends his taunts recognizing His Deity and defends Him against the other.
He speaks to the confessing thief, *"Truly I say to you, today you will be with Me in Paradise."* [2]

His words reverberate in my heart still.
He speaks to His mother, *"Woman, this is your son."* **And, to His disciple, John,**
"This is your mother." [3]
My sinless substitute is the only perfect sacrifice for all mankind.
He cries in agony for His loss of Divine fellowship, His Father's Holy Presence.
"My God, My God, why have You forsaken Me." [4]

His words speak of suffering I cannot understand, but these are not the only words I hear.
"I thirst." He shares. I think not for a drop of wine, but for the lost souls He is dying to secure.
Who is this Man? The sign nailed above His head reads, "Jesus, King of the Jews."
Jesus, Son of God, and man is He. Fulfilling prophecy, hear Him now as He speaks.
His sacrifice was complete. *"Father into Your hands I commit My spirit."* [5]
Then, He gives His Victory cry. *"It is finished."* [6]

His words bring hope for all those who will hear and listen.
His sacrifice and suffering were done. The Father's judgment against all mankind satisfied.
Jesus's body taken down from the cross, was wrapped and laid in a borrowed tomb to rest.
Oh, but Jesus was not done, no indeed. He did not say, "I am finished."
No, He rose again and was seen, and commissioned His followers and us to, **"Go and Tell."** [7]
Now for all who have His sacrifice applied, He will return and gather them home for the Eternal Day.

April 25, 2019

Father, I heard Dave Early remind us of Jesus' last words that Easter Sunday. Equally reminding us that Jesus' words were not that He was finished. No, death did not hold Him. His words were His victory song. He had finished the plan of my salvation and restoration. He conquered death and the grave for me. If I could be, I would be finished with sin, Abba, but I know that cannot happen in my mortality. So, Abba, grant me the wisdom, the strength, and the energy to follow hard after You. Then, when I at last put on immortality, I will be finished with sin, but not be finished, just living sin free in Eternity. Amazing Abba. With gratitude and love always, and really always. Your world without end. Amen.

Love and Obedience

You gave John and me two miracles: a daughter and a son.
They arrived as all babies do who gestate well, naked, fragile, crying, and needy.
So, we loved them instantly and wanted to provide for their safety and wellbeing.
Totally clueless with the first You helped us learn to care for her.
We were better with the second but even then, what we had learned was at times insufficient.
They took maximum effort giving little in return for they were just infants.
But our bond with them was unbreakable and we cherished every little smile, sound, and movement.

Oh, but they didn't remain infants and soon left toddler years behind too.
Then, our job was no longer feeding, changing, and burping them but something far more.
Now we had to teach them how to live and care for themselves.
Educate them, instruct them in Your will, rear them as giving loving beings.
The only guidance we had was what we had been given.
Our support and advice came from multiple generations of family and church.
We sought to give them knowledge of You and Your word to sustain them throughout their lives.

Today, Abba, I am thinking of You as our Sovereign Parent.
Thinking of how You see us, how much You gave and what You asked in return.
How You selected Abraham and Sarah, Isaac and Rebekah, and Jacob, Leah, and Rachel.
Really all their generations and what You gave and expected from them.
I think of the flood and Noah and his Mrs., their sons and daughters-in-law.
I've read how You cared for all of them in their hostile environs and brought them through.
Yet, I can't forget their weaknesses and failures. <u>Even so</u>, You never let them go.

I think of Joseph, Jacob's son, sold into slavery by his own jealous brothers.
I ponder Joseph's harsh years in slavery then prison when he was innocent.
Yes, Joseph was not abandoned by You but prepared to perform great good.
Joseph saved his father and brothers bringing them down to Egypt free and welcomed.
I think of four-hundred years of Egyptian enslavement for Jacob's now Israel's family.
Yet, I remember that during this time they grew into a nation and Moses was born.
He a babe condemned to die who thrived in Pharaoh's palace.

Moses, Israel's deliverer, a murderer, an outcast, a vagabond who fled.
Prince of Egypt turned fugitive a shepherd in Midian for Jethro, his father-in-law.
Then a man of eighty and slow of speech You called him out to serve You from a burning bush.
I remember Moses and Aaron's struggle with Pharaoh to let Israel go free.
I think about the nine plagues You brought down and the suffering.
The awful dark night of the final plague, the lamb sacrifices, and the meals with bitter herbs.
The night the death angel came to take the life of all first born from the palace to the stables.

I remember this night called Passover for all of Israel's firstborn were spared.
For Death passed over every house where the blood of a perfect lamb covered the door.
Pharaoh let them go, once seventy plus people now more than two million strong.
You freed them and took them out and kept and fed them as they sojourned home.
You were taking them to the land of Father Abraham You promised to him and his descendants.
You cared for them as their loving Creator and more, their God and tender Father.
You gave them manna and their clothes and shoes did not wear out in forty years of wandering.

You lead them by day in a pillar of Cloud and with a pillar of Fire at night.
When Pharaoh chased after them to bring them back to Egypt into slavery,
You stood between Israel and Pharaoh and his mighty chariots.
You opened up for Israel a means of escape drying up the Red Sea.
And when they had safely crossed You released Pharaoh to chase after them.
Then You covered the mighty chariots and men with the Red Sea destroying the enemy of Israel.
Yet, what was it that You asked of Your creation, Your chosen, Your children?

I think it was the same we asked of our own children.
Just two things You asked of them and us.
Love in return for the love You lavishly poured out on them.
Obedience to keep them well and prosper them in the land You had prepared for them.
Yes, I think this all we asked of our own children as we prepared their hearts to choose You.
Love as it sacrifices and gives good things, obedience as it protects and serves.
It worked so well when they were young and as they grew for the most part too.

Yet, in love and obedience our ancestors and their leaders often failed.
The Bible details their apostasy as they turned to other gods.
No, not gods for there is no other god beside You.
For what they worshiped, they fashioned from wood or poured out from molten metal.
Israel's children willingly gave up gold jewelry so Aaron could mold a golden calf for them to call god.
They were set apart to worship You, yet they turned away to worship an inanimate object.
Even judged for their sin they didn't learn to adore and worship You alone.

This is their reoccurring history and legacy, a cycle they couldn't break.
They insanely graved to be like the Canaanites You despised.
They worshiped and sacrificed to man-made idols killing animals and their children too.
They reveled in sexual immorality wanting and doing all the pagan nation's around them practiced.
They couldn't love as You loved them and earned judgment for their disobedience.
This is our legacy too, but You did not leave us to this never-ending cycle of abominations.
You sent Jesus to be the perfect blood sacrifice to cover our sin so death can pass over us.

On this Good Friday, Abba, I think of Jesus' first coming, His love, teachings, and miracles.
Once again, I see divine Love and all it gives and what that Love sacrificed.
I chill as I remember Christ's unwarranted suffering for He did nothing to deserve crucifixion.
I understand that divine Holiness had a plan to stop the cycle of sin and animal sacrifice.
I know that all Christ suffered, and His cruel crucifixion was the final required blood sacrifice.
Christ and He alone could stop the destructive cycle and open the path for us to Heaven.
Christ announced His victory over sin and death from His cross, *"**It is finished.**"*

Now all who believe in Christ and accept the payment of His blood for their sin have eternal life in Him.

His sacrifice became our gift of salvation and eternity in heaven.

Jesus' love and obedience paid for our sin so we can end our cycle of sinning and judgment.

Christ set us free from the just judgment of our sins by taking it on Himself.

Yes, He was crucified for our sins once upon a Friday now called Good Friday.

He was hastily, mournfully buried in a borrowed tomb, but He did not stay amongst the dead.

No, Jesus took up His life and is alive forevermore and has prepared a place for each of His children.

Jesus Christ's first coming saw His death, but it was not the end for Him or us.

When we apply His death and resurrection to our sin the end of our mortal life begins our eternal life.

We who die in Christ will be raised to eternal life in Him.

What is planted mortal and decaying becomes immortal and forever young and whole.

Earth is but a lifetime, eternity is life forever in the eternal city of God.

Christ Jesus asks, **"Why won't you choose life in Me. I've paid Your sin debt and will set you free."**

Look to Jesus, He is the only path that leads to the Promised Land, no not Canaan but heaven.

Abba, it is Good Friday and I sit here with so many thoughts and emotions flooding through my heart and mind as I try to focus on all the Holy Spirit directs. I type words to try to see what is pouring out of me, yet it isn't enough. I want to not just chronicle history but to praise You for all of it. You knew when You created Adam and Eve where that would lead. Yet, Your whole and perfect earth wasn't enough for You to enjoy with Jesus and the Holy Spirit. No, You wanted mankind to share Your great and awesome love, despite how You knew we would treat it.

Somehow, and I am grateful, that those of Your creation who do come to know You are enough. That You delight in us and cherish us despite our imperfections and our questionable choices we make without seeking Your will. My soul is restless inside of me. These words are not enough this year. It isn't what I thought to write. Yet, Holy Father, it is what has come out of my heart and mind. If it isn't satisfying to You Father, then I want more. If it is enough, give me Your peace. Today is a cold Good Friday, yet I am warm in my house. I am sharing this day with You, because it is who I have become, a seeker of Good Friday communion with Christ in His death, burial, and resurrection.

I truly want to be wholly Yours Abba. I want to return Your love and be obedient to Your will. I want to live above my circumstances in Your peace. I want to be grateful and satisfied with all You have provided me. I want to be joyful and hopeful despite wars, weather, violence, illness including Covid 19 and the total chaos of the sinful world I live in. I want to be Your beloved daughter in whom You delight. I want only to adore and worship You this Good Friday, this Easter, and when these days are past, I still want to adore and worship You with each breath. I want to bring You joy and gratitude all the days of my life. Your world without end, Abba, Amen.

Good Friday 2020

The Tomb and the Stone

The rich man, Joseph, spared no expense to have his tomb carved.
The stone mason prepared it meticulously with a massive stone to cover the entrance.
Oh, but Joseph never used the tomb for he lent it to Jesus.
Jesus of Nazareth had been worshiped as King with palms and Hosannas.
Yet, stood falsely accused and tried. Pontius Pilate found Him guiltless but feared the priests and people.
So, he condemned Jesus to be crucified, had Him beaten, and washed his hands of Him.
Jesus beaten, tortured, spit upon, and humiliated was nailed to a cross.
There He suffered and died giving His life for the sin of the world.
He saved a repentant thief dying beside him, granting him forgiveness and Paradise.
With Jesus' last breath He forgave us too with, **"It is finished."** [1]

What did Jesus mean you ask?
Since Adam and Eve, sin required a blood sacrifice for it to be atoned.
Until that day animal sacrifice had been the way but had to be repeated three times a day.
Jesus, God's Son's sacrifice was once, and applied to any who would believe and accept His gift.
So, God accepted Jesus' sacrificial death as the final atonement for all sin.
Our Jesus crucified did not simply die but control His death giving up His life.
Our Jesus, Son of God, fulfilled all the prophecies in His life and death.
Not a bone in His body was broken but a spear did pierce His side.
His bloody lifeless body was hastily taken down from the cross and laid in Joseph's tomb.

The massive stone cover was rolled in place by muscled men on that Friday evening.
Then it was sealed by Pilate's order and guarded by well-trained Roman or temple soldiers.
Jesus' disciples and followers didn't understand and mourned His death.
They feared all was lost and that their lives would be forfeited next.
They hid in fear, but Jesus did not linger in the borrowed tomb.
Death could not keep Him for He went into hell and set the captives free.
He conquered sin and death for all who would believe.
Sunday sunrise came and the women went to anoint His body in the tomb.
The massive stone, the governor's seal, and the guard would block their care.
Who would remove the massive stone for them?

We too may have a massive stone blocking our way to Jesus.
Unsaved the sin in our lives is a massive stone to the pardon offered by Jesus.
Doubts about God, Jesus, and the Holy Spirit seal us tight inside our tomb.
Our life's circumstances, hurts, bitterness post guards at our tomb to keep us in.
So, who will remove the stone?
The women arriving at the tomb found the guards gone and the stone removed.
An angel there spoke to them, *"Do not be afraid. He is not here. He has risen as He said."*
Oh, yes, they didn't need the stone removed for it was already gone.
All the barriers to God had been removed, Jesus had risen, and He would soon come to them. [2]
This Jesus will do for us too if we confess our sin, our doubts, our bitterness.

Satan would have you believe lies and half-truths to make you believe that the Bible is not true.
He will whisper that what we do is fine, and not <u>sin</u> as we should enjoy our mortal lives.
He will speak <u>doubts</u> as to who God, Jesus, and the Holy Spirit are and what they can do.
He uses <u>bitterness</u> as darts to harm our spirits in order to keep us trapped inside our lives, our tombs.
It's true we cannot escape mortal death, but that is just our bodies.
Yes, beloved, we are eternal beings wrapped in mortal bone and flesh.
Death frees all from mortal days, but then the eternal soul and spirit move on to eternal bodies.
Those trapped in unbelief will rise to eternal damnation to a place called hell.
Those who believe in Jesus will rise to eternal life with the Trinity in the heavenlies. [3]
Salvation is a free gift from God paid in full by Jesus our Advocate, God's only Son.

You see the women went in hope to the tomb not knowing how to have the stone removed.
What they discovered there was the guard, the seal, and stone were already gone.
Jesus was no longer there; death did not have the power to keep Him. He arose forevermore. [4]
His borrowed tomb is now an opened doorway to heaven for all eternity.
When you believe and place your faith in Jesus, you'll find the stone to your tomb is gone too.
It is Satan's lies that keep unbelievers trapped in tombs falsely believing their stone is a barricade.
Say the sinner's prayer, beloved, confess your sin, and all doubt and bitterness will be removed.
Jesus waits with open arms to receive and forgive you and offers you peace the world cannot perceive.
Death is real, beloved, but so is eternity. Where will you spend eternity?
The stone to your tomb has already been removed, rise, and walk through it and find Jesus.

Easter Sunday
April 12, 2020

Abba, this was not the text of Jerry Neal's sunrise sermon today, but it is what filtered through to me from the Holy Spirit. I watched it pajamaed and sleepy sheltering in place. The world is indeed in crisis because of Covid-19, but the Holy Spirit has given me much to write about this last week, and He, You, Abba, and Jesus are my peace. Jesus speaks life into the covenant You have made with Your beloved. Help now any unbelief that whispers to me, tame my fears, rebuke doubt for You are Holy and sovereign. Whereas I don't know how Covid-19 ends, I know the Author and I am living in divine peace. Resurrection weekend is for me the greatest remembrance day, and this year it was made special because Jared proposed to Heather and she said, "Yes."

So, he has a bride-to-be and a new daughter, Nora. Next Easter, Abba, I pray that we all, the Fegans, Weavers, Millers, et al will all gather together. Thank you for the Holy Spirit's success in reaching souls during this pandemic. Your world without end, Abba. Amen.

Unstoppable Love!

Abba, You created the universe and our little planet in it.
The divine love of the Trinity gave mankind a garden home on this little planet called Earth.
You placed our first parents, Adam and Eve, Your unique creations, in Eden: their garden home.
You gave them beauty and perfection and a personal relationship with You to share therein.
Obedience was all You asked, for love and worship came easily for them.
Yet, You knew they'd disobey, and You'd have to rescue them.

Ah, yes, Abba, the plan of salvation and restoration came along with creation.
Their act of disobedience was eating the only fruit in the garden forbidden to them.
Disobedience that cost them their innocence and sinlessness and easy garden life.
The first animal sacrifice, by You, clothed them, but did not clear their debt of sin.
Did not clear the sin debt for their children, their descendants, us, or the people Your love foresaw.
Yes, from the beginning You love made the plan for our salvation and restoration.

Abba, Your patience with Your creation, mankind, still amazes me.
You allowed generation after generation the opportunity to obey and serve You.
Most did not, yet You were loving, faithful and patient.
The world in Noah's day was so corrupt, Your patience waned.
You found only one man amongst the many to be faithful and obedient.
He built an ark according to Your design and plan.

This was no easy task with hand tools and the ridicule of the sinful men who mocked him.
Yet, Your faithful servant Noah warned them of Your coming wrath.
A giant ship Noah built inland where no body of water could be seen.
Your love, patience, and Noah's persistent workmanship and worship took one-hundred years of building.
How difficult it must have been for You to see Your creation that You loved so unrepented.
At last, the ark was finished and stocked by Noah, his wife, their three sons and their wives.

It was ready for the animals You called to the ark for the survival of both mankind and beast.
Noah's preaching was finished, and with all on board You closed the door and opened up Earth's floodgates.
The ark was the cradle of the rebirth of mankind and the replenishing of the world.
The ark floated and all except eight died in the world wide flood.
Sadly, sin in Your creation, did remain and disembarked from the ark. [1]
Your love remained unchanged, and the plan of salvation and restoration was not finished.

In time, You called a man named Abram to separate himself from his father's family.
Called him to go to Canaan land and serve You there.
You gave him and his wife, Sarah, Isaac, in their advanced age the son You so long promised them. [2]
Isaac later had twin sons, Esau and Jacob, who were not at all alike.
Esau was the father of the Edomites, and Jacob later called Israel the Israelites.
Now Jacob had twelve sons and ten conspired to sell the eldest son of Rachel, a dreamer, into slavery.

Yes, they sold Joseph to the Ishmaelites for twenty shekels, and they sold him in Egypt to Potiphar.
There through slavery and false imprisonment, Your hand was stayed upon him, and he flourished.
In time, through divine dream interpretation, he became governor in Egypt.
Famine came to the land and Joseph's food plan saved the Egyptians and Israel's family. [3]
Now Joseph's plan not only saved his family but shows Your care in human affairs.
For by saving them, You thwarted Satan's plan and preserved the lineage of Your only Son, Jesus.

So, the plan of salvation and restoration was unstoppable as Satan could not end Jesus' family.
Mankind flourished yet again with opportunities to love, serve, worship, and obey You.
King and kingdoms came and went, and man gravely sinned, but You did not destroy them all ever again.
In time, the plan of salvation and restoration became flesh according to many prophecies.
Abba, from You, planned from the beginning, from the Trinity, Jesus came.
He gave up heaven and being served by angels; gave up His relationship in the Trinity to serve and save.

Jesus put on mortal flesh but remained divine to be born to the virgin Mary and her husband Joseph.
They were both descendants of the royal family of David. [4]
Yes, from the Davidic line that You promised would have an eternal son to reign from David's throne. [5]
Abba, Jesus, Your only Son, remained God, but was now also human like us.
Centuries had passed since creation and Jesus came in the time of the Romans and crucifixion.
Yes, Abba, Jesus obediently came in love, but the plan of salvation and restoration was not finished. [6]

Satan put in the heart of Herod a murderous plot to destroy male infants to blot out Your son.
Even before Jesus' birth, You knew this day would come and Jeremiah wrote about it.
"A voice is heard in Ramah, mourning and great weeping, Rachel weeping for her children
And refusing to be comforted, because they are no more."[7]
But You protected Jesus for all mankind through Your obedient servants, Mary and Joseph.
No, Satan could not stop or even thwart the plan of salvation and restoration.

Your word tells us little of Jesus' family life except to tell us that He was sinless.
So, Jesus' public baptism and recognition of His deity I hold very dear.
Jesus came to Jordan and was baptized there by His cousin, John.
John was reluctant to do this because he knew that Jesus should be baptizing him.
But Jesus put him at ease, **"Let it be so now; it is proper for us to do this to fulfill all righteousness."**
Then, when Jesus came up out of the water, Abba, You recognized Jesus and His coming ministry.

Heaven opened, and Jesus saw the Spirit of God descending like a dove and alighting on Him.
And You spoke from heaven, **"This is My Son, <u>whom I love</u>; with Him I am well pleased."**
Here, Abba, we can see the Trinity, the One in Three, all at the same time and place.
Father, Jesus, Your only Son, and the Holy Spirit, separate beings, yet the same, the Divine Trinity.
How very special this moment must have been for Jesus and cherished throughout His ordeal to come.
For next Your Spirit led Jesus into the wilderness to be tempted by Satan, our enemy. [8]

Now it seems Jesus fasted for forty days and nights to prepare for his ministry and was hungry.
Then the tempter, Satan, came to Him and said to challenge His power.
"If you are the Son of God, tell these stones to become bread."
Jesus did answer him from Your holy word, **"It is written: 'Man shall not live on bread alone,**
But on every word that comes from the mouth of God.'" Then the devil took him to Jerusalem
And the highest point of the temple. *"If you are the Son of God,"* he said, *"throw yourself down."* [9]

Now here is a sad point but Satan too can quote or misquote scripture for his own gain.
"For it is written: "'He will command His angels concerning You, and they will lift You up
In their hands, so that You will not strike Your foot against a stone.'"
Jesus answered him, **"'It is also written: 'Do not put the LORD your God to the test.'"**
Then, Satan took Jesus to a high mountain and showed Him the splendor of all the world.
"All this I will give you," he said, *"if you will bow down and worship me."* [10]

Now I understand the world was Satan's to offer and Jesus could co-reign with him without dying.
Indeed, Satan, in his three temptations, tempted Jesus the same way he does us.
All temptations come from the lust of the flesh, the lust of the eyes, and the pride of life.
But we, by knowing and applying Your word, Abba, have the same power to resist Satan.
Jesus said to him, **"Away from me, Satan! For it is written: 'Worship the LORD your God**
And serve Him only.'" *Then Satan left Him, and angels came and attended Him.* [11]

Abba, Satan tried to kill Jesus as an infant and tempted
Him to sin as a man so He couldn't be our sinless sacrifice.
Jesus fully man could be tempted, but like us did not have to give into temptation and sin.
"No temptation has overtaken you except what is common to mankind.
And God is faithful; He will not let you be tempted beyond what you can bear.
But when you are tempted, He will also provide a way out so that you can endure it. [12]
Jesus succeeded against our common enemy, so the plan of salvation and restoration continued.

After Jesus' confrontation with Satan and victory over his plot to turn Jesus away from the plan,
Jesus began His ministry by selecting twelve men to disciple for their part in the completed plan. [13]
Twelve disciples but many more followers who believed in Him but didn't understand the plan.
They saw Jesus and expected Him through His divine power to conquer the Romans.
They expected that He would set them free from oppression and rule over them as an earthly king.
Expected His power to keep them from hunger, illness, and to restore life as only He could.

Ah, but Jesus' kingdom wasn't of this world, not temporal, but eternal.
He came to restore our love relationship with the Trinity and to restore creation.
The disciples probably even expected the sacrificial system of the temple to continue.
This, too, He came to end by being the only sacrifice that could take away all of our sin.
The blood of lambs and bulls could never suffice to restore what deceit took in the garden.
You, Holy Father, required Jesus' obedience and submission to be our ultimate sacrifice.

Each day of Jesus' three year ministry to train His disciples and followers, He knew the cost.
He knew the time, the location, Judas, His betrayer, and the falling away of His followers.
Still, He continued to love them like no other, perform miracles, teach them, and to pray.
He was Your son, a person of the Godhead and He needed to pray. How much more we?
He knew on that Palm Sunday that the crowd who was waving palm branches before Him and shouting,
"Hosanna!" would later rally around the priests who wanted Him dead and shout, "Crucify Him!" [14]

Being fully God and fully man He shared a last supper with His disciples and His betrayer.
He washed their feet, always the example of serving and caring, He even washed Judas' feet.
I often don't remember that Satan in Judas shared in this meal too.
Jesus taught them to remember His coming sacrifice by sharing bread, His body, and the cup, His blood.
Centuries of waiting for the time to come, for all prophecies regarding Him to be fulfilled unfolded.
Yet, Jesus looked toward heaven and prayed for His disciples, followers, and me that night. [15]

"Father, the hour has come. Glorify Your Son, that Your Son may glorify You.
For You granted Him authority over all people that He might give eternal life to all those
You have given Him. Now this is eternal life: that they know You,
The only true God, and Jesus Christ, whom You have sent.
I have brought You glory on earth by finishing the work You gave Me to do.
And now, Father, glorify Me in Your presence with the glory I had with You before the world began.

I have revealed You to those whom You gave Me out of the world.
They were Yours; You gave them to Me, and they have obeyed Your word.
Now they know that everything You have given Me comes from You.
For I gave them the words You gave Me, and they accepted them.
They knew with certainty that I came from You, and they believed that You sent Me.
I pray for them. I am not praying for the world, but for those You have given Me, for they are Yours.

All I have is Yours, and all You have is Mine. And glory has come to Me through them.
I will remain in the world no longer, but they are still in the world, and I am coming to You.
Holy Father, protect them by the power of Your name, the name You gave Me,
So that they may be one as We are One. While I was with them, I protected them
And kept them safe by that name You gave Me.
None has been lost except (Judas) the one doomed to destruction so that Scripture would be fulfilled.

"I am coming to You now, but I say these things while I am still in the world,
So, that they may have the full measure of My joy within them.
I have given them Your word and the world has hated them,
for they are not of the world any more than I am of the world.
My prayer is not that You take them out of the world but that You protect them from the evil one.
They are not of the world, even as I am not of it.

Sanctify them by the truth; Your word is truth.
As you sent Me into the world, I have sent them into the world.
For them I sanctify Myself, that they too may be truly sanctified.
"My prayer is not for them alone.
I pray also for those who will believe in Me through their message,
That all of them may be one, Father, just as You are in Me, and I am in You.

May they also be in Us so that the world may believe that You have sent Me.
I have given them the glory that You gave Me, that they may be one as We are One—
I in them and You in Me—so that they may be brought to complete unity.
Then the world will know that You sent Me and have loved them even as You have loved Me.
"Father, I want those You have given Me to be with Me where I am, and to see My glory,
The glory You have given Me because You loved Me before the creation of the world.

"Righteous Father, though the world does not know You,
I know You, and they know that You have sent Me.
I have made You known to them,
and will continue to make You known in order that the love
You have for Me may be in them and that I Myself may be in them." [16]
Thank you, Abba, Jesus, and the Holy Spirit for remembering me even on this dark night.

Abba, when Jesus said to glorify Him so He could glorify You,
It seemed He was asking for the power to finish the final part of His task
And to return to the love and the glory You shared before You created the world.
Through Jesus' sojourn and task on earth He had shown His elect, me, Your divinity.
Jesus said, "I will remain in the world no longer and I am coming home to You."
The depth of this unstoppable love is hard to understand.

But I left out, *"but they are still in the world"* and He reminded You that His followers would remain.
And He asked You to leave us here in the world but protect us by Your great name.
He asked You to allow us to *"have the full measure of My joy within them."*
He asked You to protect us not just from the world, but from Satan.
"Sanctify them by the truth, by Your word." He asked.
Then, He spoke of me, *"for all those who will believe in Me."*

He prayed that we would all share in this great love and the unity of the Trinity.
Share in the love that created us in a relationship we can only glimpse here in the world.
He spoke of wanting us to be with Him and see His glory where He is, which is heaven.
His prayer reminds me of all He gave up to come here and become human.
I see how strong the love was that was shared before the world began.
Jesus' last supper ended and then He went to the garden where He prayed.

Was the Garden of Gethsemane a battleground for Jesus that night?
It is clear Jesus wholly God and wholly man had a great spiritual battle to fight there.
He took the eleven to the garden with Him, and eight He had stay at a distance.
He took three, Peter, James, and John, with Him, for He was troubled and sorrowful.
"My soul is overwhelmed with sorrow to the point of death. Stay here and keep watch with Me."
Going a little further, He fell with his face to the ground and prayed to You, His Father.

"My Father, if it is possible, may this cup be taken from Me. Yet not as I will, but as You will."
He returned and found them sleeping and told them to pray so as not to fall into temptation.
Perhaps it is here, Abba, that You answered Jesus' prayer and sent an angel with Your answer.
For an angel from heaven appeared to Him and strengthened Him, for we know Your answer was "No."
And, being in anguish, He prayed more earnestly,
And His sweat was like drops of blood falling to the ground. [17]
Oh, the cost of this unstoppable love was so much to ask, yet Jesus was strengthened to finish the task.

Jesus' second prayer seems to be acceptance. **"My Father if it is not possible for this cup
to be taken away unless I drink it, may Your will be done."** He found His disciples asleep again.
Is it possible then that His third prayer was for more strength
To complete the plan of salvation and restoration?
**"Jesus offered up prayers and petitions with fervent cries and tears to the One who could
Save Him from death, and He was heard because of His reverent submission."** [18]
Yes, Abba, He was given the strength to overcome any human weakness in Himself and finish His arduous task.

Now I pause, Abba, to think what if. What if Jesus hadn't finished the plan?
I would clearly have no means of salvation and restoration for I am not worthy of it in myself.
But, what of Jesus? What if He hadn't obeyed? What if He hadn't completed the plan?
Since He was now human, would He too have spent eternity separated from You?
This certainly would have been the hope of Satan, but he is strangely silent in these hours.
Did Satan and his demons hold their breaths and silently hope the plan would be stopped?

"Jesus, for the joy set before Him endured the cross, scorning its shame,
and sat down at the right hand of the throne of God." [19]

Jesus then woke His disciples for the son of perdition, Judas, came to betray Him with a most unholy kiss.
I believe, Abba, that this night time garden scene became suddenly darker when Satan and his demons came.
Surely Satan wanted to watch and gloat over Jesus' arrest and demons kept company with the heartless mob.
Yet, in this time, I see the love and power of heaven and one last miracle.
Jesus, knowing all that was going to happen to Him, went out and asked them, **"Who is it you want?"**

Herein, Abba, is the power I didn't see for a long time in the story of Your son's arrest.
"Jesus of Nazareth," they replied.
"I am He," Jesus said. When Jesus said, **"I am He,"** they drew back and fell to the ground.
So, Judas, a detachment of soldiers, and officials from the temple carrying torches, lanterns, and weapons
Fell to the ground when Jesus identified Himself. Mostly certainly Satan and the demons fell down too!
Confusion reigned when Peter struck Malchus, the high priest's servant with his sword and cut off his ear!
Ah, but then, Jesus rebuked Peter for trying to intervene with the plan of salvation and restoration.

Jesus commanded Peter, **"Put your sword away! Shall I not drink the cup the Father has given Me?"**
Then one last act of love, a miracle of healing, Abba, for Jesus even in this dark hour restored Malchus' ear.
Then Jesus allowed Himself to be led away without rescue from heaven so the plan could proceed. [20]
Now, Abba, what I want to note is that Jesus had escaped such confinement before.
"They took Him to a cliff to throw Him off and Jesus walked away through the crowd and left." [21]
"At this they tried to seize Him, but no one laid a hand on Him, because His hour had not yet come." [22]

"Do you think that I cannot appeal to My Father, and He will at once
Send Me more than twelve legions of angels?
But how then should the Scriptures be fulfilled, that it must be so?" **At that hour Jesus said to the crowds,**
"Have you come out as against a robber, with swords and clubs to capture Me?
Day after day I sat in the temple teaching, and you did not seize Me.
But all this has taken place that the Scriptures of the prophets might be fulfilled."
Then all the disciples left Him and fled. [23]

Next, Abba, came Jesus' illegal secret night time trial before Caiaphas and the Sanhedrin.
They couldn't find two false witnesses to be able to condemn Jesus.
So, Jesus, grants them what they need to condemn Him. In truth, He just confesses His true identity.
So, they charged Him with blasphemy, spit in His face, slapped Him, and sentenced Him to death.
However, under Roman law, they had no authority to kill Him, so they took Jesus to Pilate.
But, Abba, the story here isn't the false trail, but Peter's predicted denial coming true.

Now during the last supper, Jesus had told them that on His account they would scatter and leave Him.
They all denied this, and impetuous Peter did later defend Jesus with his sword.
"Simon, Simon, Satan has asked to sift all of you as wheat. But I have prayed for you, Simon,
that your faith may not fail. And when you have turned back, strengthen your brothers."
Peter replied, *"Even if all fall away on account of you, I never will."* **"Truly I tell you,"** Jesus answered,
"This very night, before the rooster crows, you will deny Me three times."

So, the ten did scatter, but Peter followed Jesus to the courtyard of Caiaphas.
Three people accused Peter of knowing Jesus and Peter denied his identification with the master each time.
Here is the poignant part of Peter's story for me, Abba.
Just as Peter was speaking, the rooster crowed. **The LORD turned and looked straight at Peter.**
Peter was that near to Jesus and remembered the words He had spoken to him:
"Before the rooster crows today, you will deny me three times." *And Peter went outside and wept bitterly.*

Even at this point, Abba, Jesus could have saved Himself, but continued to allow His crucifixion.
So, Jesus was taken to the Roman governor, Pontius Pilate, for trial, where He was found innocent.
This displeased the priests and crowd, so finding that Jesus was a Galilean, Pilot sent Him to Herod to be tried.
Now Jesus wouldn't answer Herod, nor did Jesus perform any sign to Herod's dismay.
So, in Herod's hands, Jesus was dressed in a purple robe, mocked, and ridiculed by Roman soldiers.
Then Jesus, in His own clothing, was returned to Pilate who really wanted nothing to do with Him.

An interesting note, Abba, that Pilate and Herod, who had been enemies, now became friends.
Pilate tried one more ploy. He let the crowd choose between releasing Jesus or the notorious Barabbas.
The temple priest stirred the crowd to demand Barabbas' release and Jesus' crucifixion.
Fearing a riot, Pilate literally washed his hands before the crowd, saying that He was innocent of Jesus' blood.
The people said, "Let His blood be on us and our children."
And so, it would be, His shed blood to condemn or set free.
Then, Pilate released Barabbas, had Jesus scourged, who he had found innocent,
and delivered Him to be crucified.

Satan surely feels like he is winning because Jesus is nearly beaten to death with a flagrum.
Jesus' wounds were so deep that His muscles were torn, and His internal organs exposed.
Jesus was dehydrated, weak from blood loss, and in shock.
Modern doctors would have found Him hard to treat.
In His condition, He could barely make it up Golgotha Hill, the site of Roman crucifixions.
The Roman soldiers compelled Simon of Cyrene to carry
His cross beam on which Jesus would be crucified.
Tortured like no other human before, Jesus was nailed to the beams and raised up to die.

Normally death from crucifixion took several days, but my Jesus was on
My cross from nine to three that Friday.
Daylight hours, noon even, yet the site of the crucifixion was unusually dark. [24]
Now let me ponder David's Psalm 22 which describes this moment
Jesus' crucifixion before there were Romans and crucifixion.
"They divided my clothes among them and cast lots for My garment." [25]
Jesus' love for His mother, even near death, was evident as He gave her care to John the Beloved. [26]
Jesus was dying for the sin of mankind, but two condemned thieves hung on either side of Him.

At first, both thieves mocked Jesus along with the soldiers and the crowd.
Later seeing the love of Jesus and His miraculous response to His tormentors, one thief believed.
He humbled himself and rebuked the other dying thief for his treatment of Jesus and asked,
"Jesus, remember me when You come into Your kingdom."
So, the humbled dying thief seeking forgiveness found unstoppable love, forgiveness, and heaven.
Jesus answered him, "Truly I tell you, today you will be with Me in paradise." [27]

One dying thief that day lost his life upon his worthy cross and so writhes in eternal death.
But the other thief found his relief in my Redeemer and gained eternal life through Jesus.
We all must make the choice to accept or reject Jesus and find eternal life or eternal death.
Now God had shrouded the land in darkness while Christ hung on the cross for me.
God, our Holy Father, could not look on the Son He loved
Because Jesus had taken on the sin of the world that day!
It seemed Jesus could withstand the pain He felt yet His separation from God was too much.

Jesus had always been One with the Father and the Holy Spirit and now He was separated from Them.
The cost of the plan of salvation and restoration was nearly paid in full.
It seems the agony of His spirit was more than the pain of His body.
His tortured mind, body, and spirit asked into the darkness surrounding Him.
"My God, My God, why have You forsaken Me?" [28]
He was innocent, but the love of sinless Jesus kept Him on my crucifixion tree!

When Jesus said from upon my deserved cross, **"I am thirsty."**
He spoke of His desire for the souls of men for which He willingly suffered and died.
Then, and only then when my dear LORD had finished all He came to do and scripture was fulfilled,
He gave up His life for no person or priest; not even the enemy could take it from Him.
He said, **"Father! Into your hands I commit My spirit."**
He then released His spirit long trapped in its earthly shell with these last words. **"It is finished."** [29]

Abba, when Jesus released His Spirit into Your hands,
three amazing things happened that are often overlooked.
At that moment, the curtain of the temple was torn in two from top to bottom.
The earth shook, the rocks split, and the tombs broke open and the bodies of many holy people
Who had died were raised to life and they went into the holy city and appeared to many people.
When the centurion and those with him who were guarding Jesus saw the earthquake
And all that had happened, they were terrified, and exclaimed, "Surely He was the Son of God!" [30]

Yes, the price of sin was paid once and for all at Calvary for all who would believe.
Christ, the Lamb of God, was the perfect chosen sacrifice indeed.
To my debt of sin His death has been applied and I have been set free
The curtain was torn because we were no longer separated from God by priests and sacrifices.
Now the Sabbath was approaching, and the Jewish leaders didn't want bodies exposed on bloody crosses.
So, Pilate granted them that the dying men's legs should be broken to speed up their deaths. [31]

Now, Abba, the Passover Lamb was not to have any of its bones broken and Jesus was our Lamb. [32]
The soldiers broke the legs of the two thieves but found Jesus' already dead.
So, a soldier pierced Jesus' side with a spear, bringing a sudden flow of blood and water.
Symbolically, the blood and water from His heart and lungs refers to cleansing and life.
The blood was to cleanse us of our sins and the water a symbol of new life in Christ.
So, scripture was fulfilled again: *"Not one of his bones will be broken."* [33]

Also, Abba, the prophet Zechariah said, *"They will look at the one they have pierced."* [34]
Joseph of Arimathea, a rich prominent member of the Sanhedrin and a secret disciple of Jesus
And Nicodemus a Pharisee of the Sanhedrin who secretly meet with Jesus at night, [35,36]
Gained Pilate's permission to bury Jesus and quickly spiced and wrapped His tortured body.
Jesus' body was placed in Joseph's new unused garden tomb and its heavy stone rolled in place.
The priests, leery of Jesus' predicted resurrection, got Pilate to seal Jesus tomb and placed a guard on it. [37]

Jesus' crucifixion day has been called **Good Friday** because it led to Jesus'
Resurrection, as He said, and His victory over death and sin which is why He came.
Jesus taught them that the Son of Man must suffer many things and be rejected by the elders,
the chief priests and the teachers of the law, and that He must be killed and after three days rise again.[38]
Now, Christ did not idly rest in His borrowed tomb,
He went into hell and set the captives free and took away with Him the keys to hell and death. [39]

Resurrection Sunday came and Mary, Jesus' mother, and the other woman found His tomb empty!
The grave could not hold our Risen LORD and King. He had risen from among the dead as He said.
There was an earthquake and an angel rolled back the heavy stone and sat on it.
The guards were like dead men because his appearance was like lightning with garments dazzling white.[40]
Now if the disciples had managed to steal Christ's body as the priest claimed,
The Roman guards would have been executed.
So, the priests may have bribed temple guards to be silent about the miraculous events at the tomb of Jesus.[41]

Now, Abba, the situation with the guards means nothing to me because I know Jesus rose from His tomb.
The angel said to the women, *"Do not be afraid, for I know that you are looking for Jesus,*
Who was crucified. He is not here; He has risen, just as He said. Come and see the place where He lay.
Then go quickly and tell His disciples: He has risen from the dead and is going ahead of you into Galilee.
There you will see Him. Now I have told you." [42]
Jesus told them this at the Last Supper too, **"But after I have risen, I will go ahead of you into Galilee."** [43]

Yes, He gained victory for me over sin, hell, and death.
He freed the captives to live in heaven for all eternity.
Freed me to live in Him while I remain on this sin restrained earth.
And, when at last, He frees my spirit and my soul from its earthly dwelling,
I will live forever there in Paradise and meet the eternal living man, once crucified as a thief.
Yes! One day time will be complete, and all gathered home will live in New Jerusalem with the Trinity.

Now, Abba, there is one more portion to the plan that I have not yet mentioned.
Jesus commissioned His followers and us to go and tell His story, so all might know and believe.
The plan of salvation and restoration was indeed complete, but all of the unsaved still needed to hear it.
Now Jesus' resurrection wasn't a secret.
He appeared to the woman at His empty tomb, His disciples, and followers.
They needed to know everything Jesus taught about the love of the Trinity,
His crucifixion, and resurrection were real.
They needed to see and hear Jesus, so He stayed for forty days after His resurrection to be near.

Then Jesus returned to heaven to advocate for His beloved children there.
Then the eleven disciples went to Galilee, to the mountain where Jesus had told them to go.
When they saw Him, they worshiped Him; but some doubted.
Then Jesus came to them and said, **"All authority in heaven and on earth has been given to Me.**
Therefore, go and make disciples of all nations, baptizing them in the name of the Father and of the Son and
of the Holy Spirit, and teaching them to obey everything I have commanded you.
And surely, I am with you always, to the very end of the age."

So, all who love and trust You, Abba, Jesus, and the Holy Spirit, must Go and Tell the gospel story.
But, let me this eve of Good Friday, remember the LORD's Table that Jesus gave the night before His death.
Jesus commanded them and so us, to remember His sacrifice by the sharing of the bread and cup.
Jesus took the bread, gave thanks and broke it, and gave it to them, saying,
"This is My body given for you; do this in remembrance of Me."
He took the cup, saying, **"This cup is the new covenant in My blood, which is poured out for you.**"*[45]*

We must Go and Tell, Abba, for so many of Your children are still lost in their sins.
This piece tells the story but there is so much more to the history of Your interactions with us the Bible tells.
I pray the deceit that clings to sinful mankind will be broken and the truth revealed.
We are Your eternal creations meant to live in eternity with You, Jesus, and the Holy Spirit.
Love made the plan of salvation and restoration unstoppable, and it is available to all.
Jesus paid the cost with His sacrifice, so it is free and just a prayer away.

This is the vision John the Beloved disciple saw and it will be here soon!
"Then I saw 'a new heaven and a new earth,' for the first heaven and the first earth had passed away,
and there was no longer any sea. I saw the Holy City, the new Jerusalem, coming down out of heaven
From God, prepared as a bride beautifully dressed for her husband.
And I heard a loud voice from the throne saying,
"Look! God's dwelling place is now among the people,
and He will dwell with them. They will be His people, and God Himself will be with them and be their God.
He will wipe every tear from their eyes. There will be no more death
or mourning or crying or pain, for the old order of things has passed away."[46]

April 1, 2021

Happy Resurrection Day!
The plan of salvation and restoration to the Trinity is indeed complete!
One day, all of the saved will eat the marriage feast prepared for us in heaven.
Then, Jesus will sit down with us, and the plan of salvation and restoration will be fulfilled.

The Wilderness, The Garden, The Cross, and The Borrowed Tomb
Four Physical and Spiritual Battles and Four Victories

The Holy Spirit said, *"Come,"* and Jesus went into the wilderness after He was baptized.
Forty days and nights Jesus fasted in the wilderness.
Here untouched by His familial responsibilities He communed in the Trinity.
Here He faced the shadow of the cross cast over Him from the creation of the world.
Yes, our Jesus was, *"The Lamb of God, slain since the foundation of the world."* [1]
Here Jesus, fully God and fully man accepted the mantle of the cross laid upon His shoulders for us.

Oh, but Jesus, fully man was hungry and our enemy came to tempt Him to sin.
Ah, yes, the deceiver had a hope, a plan, to negate Jesus' role as Savior.
If Satan could get God's only son to sin, the plan of salvation would be destroyed.
Yes, tempt the hungry man of flesh and bone to prove His deity was his simple plan.
If the One on whom mankind's salvation fell failed, then mankind would be forever trapped in sin.
Satan's victory would secure mankind to his demonic world and perhaps he'd gain Jesus too!

Now when the tempter came to Him, he said,
"If You are the Son of God, command these stones to become bread."
But Jesus answered, **"It is written, 'Man shall not live by bread alone,**
but by every word that proceeds from the mouth of God.'"
Then the devil took Him up into the holy city, Jerusalem, set Him on the pinnacle of the temple,
And twisting the scripture said to Him, "If You are the Son of God, throw Yourself down.
For it is written: 'He shall give His angels charge over you,
And they will bear You up, lest you dash your foot against a stone.' "

Jesus said to him, **"It is written, 'You shall not tempt the LORD your God.'"**
Then for the third time, the devil took Him up on an exceedingly high mountain,
And showed Him all the kingdoms of the world and their glory.
And he said to Him, "All these things I will give You if You will fall down and worship me."
Then Jesus said to him, **"Away with you, Satan! For it is written,**
'You shall worship the LORD your God, and Him only you shall serve.'"

Then the devil left Him, and behold, angels came and ministered to Him. [2]
So, Jesus won the physical and spiritual battle of the wilderness for Himself and us.
His relationship with His Father and the Holy Spirit was still secure.
Then Jesus returned in the power of the Spirit to Galilee, and news of Him went out. [3]
His example to us is clear, *"Know the truth of the Father's word and it will set you free."* [4]
Jesus won the victory over temptation for Himself and us.

Jesus often went to the Garden of Gethsemane to pray in the shadow of the cross.
The garden was located on Mount Moriah, the site of Abraham's sacrifice of Isaac.
Also called Golgotha, this site was the place where Rome crucified its non-Roman criminals.
This place which Jesus favored for prayer was also called the Mount of Olives.
It is in the Kidron Valley, which has an established path used to escape from Jerusalem.
Solomon built the temple here that God designed during David's reign.

This night of prayer was like no other.
Jesus had come to pray here to His Father for another means of salvation for mankind.
Prayed three times for the bitter cup of crucifixion to be unnecessary.
Prayed in such agony that blood tainted His sweat during His fervent prayer.
He prayed, "Abba, Father, all things are possible for You.
Take this cup away from Me; nevertheless, not what I will, but what You will. [5]

Jesus' night of intercessory prayer for Himself and us ended in His sweet surrender.
Jesus surrendered Himself to be crucified for all mankind.
Then an angel appeared to Him from heaven, strengthening Him. [6]
Jesus then went, awakened His disciples, and took them to meet Judas, His betrayer.
Now Satan came to the garden that night too inside of Judas, yes, he, the evil fallen angel came.
So, Judas, as pre-arranged, betrayed Jesus with a kiss and with lying lips said, "Greetings, Rabbi." [7]

Chaos came to the garden that night where Jesus had often prayed in peace.
A detachment of troops and officers from the chief priest and Pharisees fell down.
Yes, men with swords, clubs, and lanterns fell down when Jesus identified Himself.
*Now when He said to them, **"I am He,"** they drew back and fell to the ground. [8]*
Shocked that they had unwillingly bowed at the name "I am" they struggled to their feet.
Seeing what was happening His disciples asked, "LORD, shall we strike with the sword?" [9]

Simon Peter, quickly drew his sword and struck the high priest's servant and cut off his right ear. [10]
"So, Jesus said to Peter, "Put your sword into its sheath.
Shall I not drink the cup which My Father has given Me? [11]
Do you not know that I can call on my Father, and He will give
Me at once more than twelve legions of angels?" [12]
And Jesus said, "Permit even this." And He touched Malchus' ear and healed him. [13]

Yes, Jesus was in control of the chaos that night even healing one who had come out against Him.
Then the disciples all fled in fear and Jesus was arrested, bound, and led to the high priest, Annas' home.
Six illegal trails, numerous beatings, mocking's, torture, and scouring, Jesus endured on that long night.
And Peter, who stayed near, did deny his Savior three times as Jesus said he would.
So, Jesus won the physical and spiritual battle in the garden that night.
Here the shadow and cloak of the cross was willingly and unshakably affixed to His shoulders for us.

Pontius Pilate, the Roman governor, found Jesus "Innocent!" and yet condemned Him to death.
Isaiah said of Jesus seven hundred years before His crucifixion, **"I gave my back to those who beat Me,**
My cheeks to those who plucked My beard; My face I did not shield from buffets and spitting." [14]
In agony, from His inhumane treatment the crossbar of His cross, my cross, was laid upon His shoulder.
Isaiah said too, **"Many were appalled at His appearance because**
He was disfigured beyond that of any man and His form was marred beyond human likeness" [15]

Jesus now had to physically struggle under the weight and pain of the cross bar to climb up Golgotha's Hill.
When He was no longer able to carry the cross bar, Simon of Cyrene was forced to carry it.
Stripped naked Jesus' wrist/hands were pierced with rusty spikes to nail Him to my crossbar.
Then He was hoisted up to my cross and His feet pierced to secure Him in my place.
He was my innocent substitute, carrying the debt of my sins that I could not pay.
Yes, Jesus, the Lamb of God, was the only one who could satisfy the cost of my redemption.

Jesus suffered physical human agony for me and spiritual agony that only He could know.
Being crucified for me He sought forgiveness for me not just those crucifying Him.
"Father, forgive them for they know not what they do." [16]
With the sin of the world, my sin, placed upon Him God could no longer look on Him.
The physical world around Jesus grew dark and stormy and Jesus lost His connection to the Trinity.
Then He cried out, *"My God, My God, why have You forsaken Me."* [17]

Does Jesus really quote David's psalm while dying, or does David reveal his vision of the Messiah's death?
David wrote Psalm 22 one-thousand years before Christ's crucifixion.
Jesus suffered it all and fulfilled the prophecies of the Messiah's death to become my Savior.
Surrendering His life to pay my debt He gave up His life to rescue me from eternal separation from my Father.
He doesn't succumb to death but gives Himself to God, *"Father into Your hands I commend My Spirit."* [18]
Then announces His victory over sin and death for all mankind. *"It is Finished."* [19]

Now the scripture tells us that when Jesus released His spirit to His Father,
That it was three o'clock and the temple priests were performing that hour's sacrifice as prescribed by Moses.
As they worked they suddenly saw the four inch thick sixty foot curtain split from top to bottom.
A supernatural act, indeed, but one that carried great significance.
You showed us, Abba, that Christ's sacrifice was the final one required and accepted for all mankind.
Showed us that Jesus Christ was now our high priest and the Aaronic earthly priesthood was finished. [20]

Satan, thinking he had killed Jesus, believed himself the victor over sinful mankind for eternity.
Mary, Jesus' mother, His disciples, and followers not understanding thought Jesus dead too.
Joseph of Arimathea and Nicodemus of the Sanhedrin placed His hastily prepared body into Joseph's tomb.
But My Savior was not *laid to rest* in death for He had much to do.
There was the thief He had to see in Paradise that day.
Captives to set free and the keys to Hades and death to claim.

Yes, Jesus' body was placed in a tomb but not until He had gained victory over the cross.
He had lived in its shadow since the foundation of the world; had accepted it as His mantle;
And had sought to be relieved from being sacrificed upon it.
Yet, He obediently and lovingly accepted the cross as the only way to save the beloved, mankind.
He enduring the suffering, torture, humiliation, and death of the cross finished His purpose.
He gained physical and spiritual victory over the cross bringing mankind salvation and restoration.

Messianic prophecies fulfilled, yes, but there was still His resurrection prophecy to fulfill.
Jesus taught them that He must suffer many things, and be rejected by the elders,
Chief priests and scribes, and be killed, and after three days rise again. [21]
He was placed in a rich man's tomb and the heavy stone covering was rolled into place. [22]
A seal was placed across the stone covering and a guard was placed to watch over His tomb.
All was quiet at the tomb from that Friday night until Sunday morning came.

Sunday, Resurrection Day, dawned and the tomb gave up the body of Jesus.
For Christ also suffered once for sins, the just for the unjust, that He might bring us to God,
Being put to death in the flesh but made alive by the Spirit. [23]
No death could not hold Him for God raised Him from amongst the dead.
Very early on Sunday morning, the women came to the tomb when the sun had risen.
And they asked themselves, "Who will roll away the stone from the door of the tomb for us?" [24]

Yes, Mary Magdalene and Mary the mother of James and Salome came to the tomb to anoint Jesus' body.
And behold, there was a great earthquake; for an angel of the LORD came and rolled back the stone.
Sitting on the stone, his countenance was like lightning, and his clothing as white as snow.
And the angel said to the women, "Do not be afraid, for I know that you seek Jesus who was crucified.
He is not here; for He is risen, as He said. Come, see the place where the LORD lay.
And go quickly and tell His disciples that He is risen from the dead.

And indeed, He is going before you into Galilee; there you will see Him.
Behold, I have told you."
So, they went out quickly from the tomb with fear and great joy and ran to bring His disciples word. [25]
Now Mary Magdalene returned to the empty tomb and Jesus met her there.
Jesus said to her, **"Woman, why are you weeping? Whom are you seeking?"**
"Sir, if You have carried Him away, tell me where You have laid Him, and I will take Him away."

Jesus said to her, **"Mary!"**
She turned and said to Him, "Rabboni!"
Jesus said to her, **"Do not cling to Me, for I have not yet ascended to My Father; but go to My brethren
And say to them, 'I am ascending to My Father and your Father, and to My God and your God.' "**
Mary Magdalene came and told the disciples that she had seen the LORD,
And that He had spoken these things to her. [26]

Jesus had now fulfilled all the prophecies of the Messiah's coming to redeem mankind.
In time, He appeared to all His disciples and restored Peter to Himself.
For forty days He stayed, comforted, commissioned, and was seen by more than five-hundred followers.
**And He said to them, "Go into all the world and preach the gospel to every creature.
He who believes and is baptized will be saved; but he who does not believe will be condemned." [27]**
And they went out and preached everywhere, the LORD working through them. [28]

Then, *while they watched, He ascended into heaven, and a cloud received Him out of their sight.
And while they looked steadfastly toward heaven as He went up, behold angels spoke to them,
"Men of Galilee, why do you stand gazing up into heaven?
This same Jesus, who was taken up from you into heaven,
Will so come in like manner as you saw Him go into heaven."
They went to Jerusalem from the Mount of Olives and awaited the anointing of the Holy Spirit.* [29]

So, it is that the borrowed tomb gave up its dead never to be used again.
Jesus's death swallowed up in victory Hades and Death.
"O Death, where is your sting? O Hades, where is your victory?" [30]
Rejoice, beloved, your sin debt is paid if you accept the payment made on your behalf.
Satan had no victory at the cross but was defeated there in the battle for your soul.
Therefore, if the Son makes you free, you shall be free indeed. [31]

Jesus, our Messiah, came and was the perfect sacrifice required to set mankind free of the penalty of sin.
By His sacrificial crucifixion He became my substitute and paid the sin debt I owed.
Confessing my sins, I was forgiven, received salvation, and my sins were forgotten by God.
The gift of salvation and restoration is free to all who will ask and seek it.
Cry out, "Father forgive me, Jesus, paid my debt, Holy Spirit come now please and dwell in me."
The cross was not the end but the means to an end. Forever and always. Your world without end. Amen.

Abba, I am not sure I was able to say what the Holy Spirit brought to my mind. Jesus faced crucifixion on the cross of Calvary from the foundation of the world because I needed Him to pay a debt that was unpayable by me. Physically and spiritually, this could never have been simple or easy for Him. Being divine He could do what no other could do but being human, He certainly had to struggle with all that it would require of Him. Thank you LORD Jesus for gaining victory over sin and death for me, for mine, and for everyone that cries out to You. I remember Your sacrifices. Forever and always, I am grateful. Your world without end and eternal life in heaven for the beloved through Jesus my Savior. Amen.

Jesus Our Messiah

Abba, You are our Loving Father, and made a covenant within the Trinity.
Your agape love for one another was to be shared with mankind.
So, You created the universe, our earth, all living things, and mankind.
Your covenant included the salvation and restoration of Your creation.
For the fall of our first parents, Adam and Eve, was already known to You.

How could it be Sweet Jesus that You were the required sacrifice for me?
"The Lamb of God, slain since the foundation of the world." [1]
Father, Your sinless holiness could not allow sin to come near so mankind needed to be redeemed.
Anointment, reparation for sin, had to be revealed and made clear.
Yes, reparation for the sin of the created would be required for them to come near.

Although we know of no covenant You made with Enoch, I want to now mention him.
For he had not the Holy Spirit as mankind can since Christ and Pentecost.
Yet, as the seventh pre-Flood patriarch he walked faithfully with You.
And Enoch walked with God; and he was not, for God took him. [2]
So, by his example we know men can be faithful and You reward Your faithful followers.

How is it with a man like Enoch that sin grew so rampant and You tolerated it so long in our world?
In time, Your patience and mercy came to an end and You unleashed Your righteous wrath.
You destroyed the world with a great Flood except for the righteous Noah and his family.
They, the remnant, You used to restart the world giving mankind a second chance.
You gave Noah the plans and the carpentry skills so he could build a massive ark.

A hundred years Noah built the ark and preached of the destruction of the world to come.
Surely there would have been room on the ark should any have heeded the warning?
Atlas, no one believed choosing sin over salvation and all died in the Flood.
So, You restarted the world over with Noah's family of eight and the living things You spared.
You made a covenant then with Noah and gave him a sign we still see.

Thus, I establish My covenant with you: Never again shall all flesh be cut off by the waters of the Flood;
Never again shall there be a Flood to destroy the earth."
And God said: "This is the sign of the covenant which I make between Me and you,
And every living creature that is with you, for perpetual generations:
I set My rainbow in the cloud, and it shall be for the sign of the covenant between Me and the earth. [3]

So, the Noahic covenant was established with Noah for all generations to come.
At times, devastating floods come to our little planet and the destruction of the waters are very evident.
In them, we see Your great power and can't imagine a worldwide Flood.
Oh, how is it that we see rainbows and fail to think of Your love for us and the rainbow covenant?
You see it when You create it and keep Your covenant though the world is as evil now as then.

Ten generations passed from Adam to Noah and ten from Noah to Abraham.
How far Your patience did stretch tolerating sin until the Abrahamic covenant!
Now I understand the Holy Spirit of the Trinity was still not given to man.
So sadly, their sons and daughters were wayward, disobedient, and evil as they chose.
Abraham too was not sinless but You found in him righteousness like no other of his time.

So, You made a covenant with him that directly blesses me.
Now the LORD had said to Abram: "Go from your country, from your family
and from your father's house to a land that I will show you.
I will make you a great nation; I will bless you and make your name great;
And you shall be a blessing. I will bless those who bless you.
I will curse any who curses you; and in you all the families of the earth shall be blessed." [4]

Abraham gratefully saw in it the promise of a son, for he and his wife, Sarah, were childless.
He saw Your favor promised as You would bless those he blessed and curse those he cursed.
So, father Abraham obeyed which is always the first step in following after You.
Then, ten years passed without the promised son and You renewed the covenant with him.
In a vision, You promised him not only a son but possession of the land of Canaan.

You told him of the enslavement of his descendants for four-hundred years in a distant land.
Told the righteous Abraham of their release coming out with many possessions.
"Do not be afraid, Abram. I am your shield, your exceedingly great reward."
Then You brought him outside his tent and said, 'Look now toward heaven,
and count the stars if you are able to number them, so shall your descendants be.'" [5]

"I am the LORD, who brought you out of Ur of the Chaldeans, to give you this land to inherit it." [6]
Now Abraham prepared a heifer, a goat, a ram, a turtledove and a pigeon for sacrifice.
Laid them out, the large animals spit in two opposing their other half, with the whole birds opposing.
You, Father, passed through this blood covenant as a smoking oven and flaming torch.
This was a sign of Your unilateral covenant with Abraham for he did not have to pass through the animals.

Now Abraham did not wait for the promised son so had a slave son, Ishmael, with a concubine.
Abraham was eighty-six when Hagar bore Ishmael to him. [7]
Then at ninety-nine You renewed the covenant with Abraham by the rite of circumcision.
This painful bloody rite for him, Ishmael, and the other males of his household was to be a reminder.
A reminder in their flesh of Your sovereignty and performed on Hebrew male infants of eight days hence.

The promised son, Isaac, was born to Sarah and Abraham when she was ninety and he one hundred.
This caused friction in the family so Hagar and Ishmael were sent away.
Even so, You kept Your promised to Ishmael, the slave son, and he became a mighty nation in his own right.
Now You tested Abraham and he proved himself worthy of being the covenant bearer.
You asked him to sacrifice Isaac to You when Isaac was still a beloved lad.

Oh, how hard and reluctantly was it for Abraham to obey? Even so he trusted Your sovereignty!
Although he loved Isaac his son, who was his legacy in the covenant blessing, he chose obedience.
Did he believe You would raise his son back to life again?
But You spared Isaac; stopped his sacrifice providing them a substitute offering, a perfect ram indeed.
Here, in this father and son relationship, a picture of the coming Messianic covenant is seen.

Abraham, the father, was going to obediently sacrifice his only son, Isaac.
Centuries later Your only son, Jesus, would come into this world as an infant.
Both fully divine and fully human He came to our dark sin filled world.
He, the Christ, our Messiah, in manhood would die in our place as the required atonement for our sins.
You spared Isaac but Your own son You would not for Jesus was the reparation for our sins.

So, Father, after Abraham, You renewed the Abrahamic covenant with Isaac and later, his son, Jacob.
Each man was the covenant bearer in his own right although they were not perfect men.
Isaac and Jacob have their own stories but their stories are sub-stories to Your greater story.
Your story, Father, speaks of love that created us and Your faithfulness to the plan to restore us.
Your story is also the story of Your son's Jesus obedience to the plan of salvation and restoration.

Jacob had twelve sons by two wives and two concubines, although Your plan was for man to have one wife.
Judah the fourth son born of the less loved wife, Leah, is in the lineage of Jesus, the Messiah.
Joseph the eleventh born by Rachel, the beloved wife, was used to save the line of Judah.
Now their stories still speak to me of Your Story, of Your Sovereignty and Covenant Keeping.
As brothers, their stories intertwine and are dependent on the other but Joseph was the better man.

Now Joseph at seventeen was immature and bash and his brothers ten despised him.
They first contrived a plot to kill him but Rueben placed him in a cistern, a plan to spare his life.
Whilst he was gone, Judah thought better than to kill their father's beloved son.
He thought a twenty shekel profit was a better plan so they sold him to Ishmaelites.
The traders took the sorrowful Joseph to Egypt and sold him there as a slave.

Meantime the brothers ten, sacrificed a goat and with it bloodied Joseph's multicolored coat.
Took it to their father Jacob who identified it and thought the worse.
So, Jacob by their deceit believed that his beloved Joseph was dead and greatly mourned his loss.
Now Joseph was not dead but a slave in house of Potiphar, the captain of Pharoah's bodyguard.
Father, You kept and blessed Joseph there and he found favor with his master Potiphar.[8]

Now many years slowly elapsed since Joseph lost his birthright when he was treacherously sold.
He became comptroller of all Potiphar owned but atlas he was not only a worthy man but handsome.
Potiphar's wife repeatedly sought Joseph to sleep with her but he refused.
"How could I do this great evil, and sin against God?" he asked. [9]
But escaping her grasp one day he left behind another coat and she cried, "Rape!"

So, Joseph was arrested and placed in prison although he'd been honorable and innocent.
Yet, even in this You did protect him for usually such an offense brought a painful death.
As a slave in prison, Joseph found favor with his jailer according to Your will for him.
In time, his gift of dream interpretation that had brought his brother's displeasure now was helpful.
He explained the meaning of the dreams of Pharaoh's imprisoned cupbearer and baker accurately.

The baker died as his dream went and the cupbearer was restored to service as his dream meant.
Now Joseph asked the cupbearer to remember him to Pharaoh to hopefully gain his release.
"For indeed I was stolen away from the land of the Hebrews;
and also, have done nothing here that they should put me into the dungeon." [10]
Oh, but the cupbearer's promise was forgotten and Joseph languished in the dungeon two more years.

Now Pharaoh had two dreams that troubled him and his wise men and magicians couldn't interpret them.
Then, by Your providence and timing the cupbearer remembered Joseph.
Pharaoh had Joseph brought from prison and Egyptianized his appearance.
Joseph acknowledging Your favor and sovereignty successfully interpreted his dreams.
Joseph also by Your will gave Pharaoh the plan to deal with the seven year drought forthcoming.

So, by Your design Joseph came to Egypt to spare many lives including the lives of his family.
Yet, he yearned for home, his father's household, and Canaan land.
But instead, according to Your great Sovereignty and plan, he was made comptroller of Egypt.
From a falsely imprisoned slave he became second in command of Egypt in just one day!
He was given Pharaoh's signet ring, fine clothes, a gold necklace, and an Egyptian wife! [11]

This wronged brother, now thirty, would never be a shepherd in his father's household.
He would not have a Hebrew wife or children or fully come to know Your great plan.
For what he could not know looking forward, we now see clearly looking backward.
For Jacob, also called Israel, the covenant bearer's progeny needed to be protected.
Yes, Judah, the one who arranged the deal that sold Joseph into slavery needed to be saved.

So, Joseph began his new life and started a family with his wife Asenath, the daughter of a priest of On!
Yet, we find that Joseph remained faithful to You, influenced his wife, and reared his sons to worship You.
Now we know that Judah's guilt made him flee from Israel's tents and extended family.
He couldn't look at his guilty brothers, serve his father, or see Joseph's brother, Benjamin, daily without pain.
So, he distanced himself by going to Adullam and marrying Shua, a forbidden Canaanite spouse.

They had three sons who grew to be worthless men who didn't know or worship You it seems.
Now a Canaanite maiden, Tamar, was given in marriage to Judah's firstborn son, Er.
Now Er displeased You and You took his life without giving Tamar a son to grow up to keep her.
Likewise, his brother Onan married her, displeased You and so You took his life.
So, Judah sent her to her father until his son, Shelah, would be old enough to marry her.

But Judah fearing that Shelah, being like his brothers, would die too did not bring about a marriage.
So, Tamar risked her life and devised a plan to trick Judah into sleeping with her hoping to have a son.
After Shua's death, she pretended to be a prostitute and Judah did go into her and she did conceive.
Judah as surety of her fee, a goat, left her his seal, cord, and staff with her.
When Judah learned of her conception, he sought to have her burned, not stoned, as was their custom.

Before she was killed she produced his surety and he recognized it and so spared her.
When Judah acknowledged them he said, "She has been more righteous than I,
Because I did not give her to Shelah my son." And he never knew her again.
Now Tamar gave birth to twin boys, Perez and Zerah and Perez is in the lineage of Christ. [12]
Then Judah returned to his father's tents and reared his and Tamar's sons amongst his people.

Selah too joined his grandfather's family for he is mentioned later with them.
It is evident that Judah's guilt over Joseph's betrayal had not allowed his life to be a happy one.
Now the drought You showed Pharoah in his dreams, Joseph by Your guidance did prepare to face.
During the seven good years of plenty in the land, Joseph collected and stored the excess grain.
Then after the second year of the famine Israel sent Judah and his brothers nine to buy grain.

They appeared before their Egyptianized brother to bargain and they did not recognize him.
Joseph though knew them and spoke through an interpreter to keep his identity safe.
Calling them spies he imprisoned them for three days and devised a plan to test them.
He wanted to see what kind of men they had become.
He wanted to know how his father, Israel, fared and what had become of his younger brother, Benjamin.

After three days, he released all but Simeon, giving them grain and secretly returning their payment.
He instructed them to return with Benjamin to prove themselves men worthy of trade not spies.
Now they found their payment returned and feared to go back to Egypt without Benjamin.
Jacob, fearing he'd now lost Simeon as well as Joseph, would not let them return to prove themselves.
But when the grain gave out, they had no other choice but to return to face the governor of Egypt!

So, Jacob let Benjamin go to Egypt but Joseph tested them further after freeing Simeon.
He lunched with them and observed his brothers' treatment of Benjamin when he was favored.
Then he sent them on their way again with grain, their doubled money returned, and his silver cup.
After a short delay, he sent men after them to return them and his cup secreted into Benjamin's bags.
Now the price of the test was to enslave the one who had his cup, so Benjamin faced enslavement.

Judah, having pledged himself to Israel to protect Benjamin, knew as they traveled what he must do.
Before Joseph, the comptroller of Egypt, he pleaded for Benjamin's release.
He offered himself as the substitute for Benjamin to be Joseph's slave in his stead.
This is the picture of Jesus, our Messiah, who became our substitute, the reparation for our sins.
Judah would take Benjamin's place and Jesus, *innocent unlike Judah*, would take our place.

Now the story of Joseph and his brothers continues for many years.
But at this time, we see him acting like our Jesus, God's obedient servant.
Although Judah and the brothers never ask for forgiveness of their betrayal of Joseph, Joseph gives it.
He identifies himself to them privately and they fear he will take revenge.
But he says to them in tears without malice, *"Please come near me."* [13]

"I am Joseph your brother, whom you sold into Egypt.
But now, do not therefore be grieved or angry with yourselves because you sold me here.
God sent me before you to preserve life for these two years the famine has been in the land,
And there are still five years in which there will be neither plowing nor harvesting.
And God sent me before you to preserve a posterity for you in the earth,
And to save your lives by a great deliverance. So now it was not you who sent me here, but God.
He has made me a father to Pharaoh, lord of all his house, and a ruler throughout all the land of Egypt." [14]

Now we know that Joseph sent wagons with his brothers when they went home to Canaan.
Coming back to Egypt with their father and their families they sojourned favorably in Goshen for many years.
Jacob, Israel, dies in Egypt and is mummified and returned to the family burial cave in Hebron.
Joseph later dies too and is mummified and makes his family swear to take his bones home.
Now as You told Abraham their descendants were eventually made slaves in Egypt for four-hundred years.

But as promised, You raised up Moses and his brother Aaron to face the Pharaoh of their time.
Through nine plagues Pharaoh refuses to let the slaves go but finally frees them after the tenth plague.
Israel's descendants obediently take Joseph's bones and many of their neighbors' possessions with them.
Sadly, due to the disobedience of the people, this journey of a few weeks took forty years.
Moses doesn't go into the promised land but Joshua leads the people in the battles for the land.

The Canaanites like the Israelites were a vast people who had to be conquered.
Under Your direction and Joshua's leadership they take much of the land starting with Jericho.
Sadly, for the Israelites, still a difficult and disobedient people, this possession is never fully realized.
After the death of Joshua and the leadership of his generation, the Israelites repeatedly sin.
As predicted, they become idol worshipers' of the Canaanites gods.

Under the leadership of Moses and Joshua, You renewed the Abrahamic covenant with the Israelites.
However, the Israelites, Your elect, break the covenant to serve You alone time and time again.
However, Joseph's bones are at last entombed at his father's property in Shechem.
Now as much as ever, if not more the Israelites need their coming Messiah.
Not only do they need Jesus, the Messiah, so does the whole of mankind.

Now we already know Abba, that a despised Canaanite, Tamar, is in Your son's lineage.
She is an Adullamite and Rahab a Canaanite from Jericho will join her as a mother in Christ's lineage.
Their stories then are threads woven into the fabric of Your story in Your restoration plan for mankind.
Rahab, the harlot, developed faith in the God of Israel from all she had heard of Him.
When Joshua sent in two spies to search out the land she protected them and asked their help.

"For we have heard how the LORD dried up the water of the Red Sea for you when you came out of Egypt.
That you utterly destroyed Sihon and Og, the two Amorite kings on the other side of the Jordan.
And as soon as we heard these things, our hearts melted; neither did there remain any more courage.
Your God, is God in heaven above and on earth beneath. Therefore, I beg you, swear to me by the LORD,
Since I have shown you kindness, that you also will show kindness to my father's house, sparing my father,
My mother, my brothers, my sisters, and all that they have, and deliver our lives from death."

So, the men answered her, "Our lives for yours, if none of you tell this business of ours.
And it shall be, when the LORD has given us the land, that we will deal kindly and truly with you."
Now, Abba, I note that the Israelites crossed the Red Sea on dry land by Your divine provision.
There You told Joshua to circumcise all the men in his charge for this had not been done in the wilderness.
During their recovery, they celebrated Passover and the manna stopped once they had eaten from the land. [15]
Next Father, Joshua met with the captain of the LORD of hosts and Jericho was taken.

During this remarkable siege Joshua, his men, with the priests' carrying the ark marched around Jericho.
They march around this eight and half acre city once a day for six days and seven times on day seven.
They were silent until the last round that day then the trumpets of the priest were blown and they shouted.
Joshua said to the people, "Shout! For the LORD has given you the city." And the thick city walls fell down.
Rahab's home on the wall was marked by a scarlet cord for her protection and was spared by You
Everything was under the ban, save her and her family and the precious metals taken for the treasury. [16]

So, Joshua and his men spared her family when You miraculously brought the walls of Jericho down.
Later she married Salmon, one of Joshua's generals and they gave life to Boaz.
Boaz, in the lineage of Christ, marries Ruth, the Moabite widow of Mahlon of the tribe of Judah.
Boaz like Judah foreshadows Jesus. Judah was willing to sacrifice his life as a substitute for Benjamin.
Boaz is the kinsman redeemer, for Ruth, as Jesus is for mankind and He as well our sinless substitute. [17]

Now Boaz and Ruth' son, Obed, fathered Jesse and Jesse fathered David who became king of the Israelites.
All five, Judah, Salmon, Boaz, Obed, and Jesse, are covenant keepers of the Abrahamic covenant.
Through Abraham and them all the world was to be blessed by the promised Messiah.
With David, You made a new covenant, the Davidic or Messianic covenant.
This covenant promise was fulfilled by Jesus, our soon returning King. [18]
God spoke through His prophet Nathan to David.

"When your days are fulfilled and you rest with your fathers,
I will set up your seed after you. I will establish the kingdom of your son Solomon .
He shall build a house for My name, and I will establish the throne of his kingdom forever.
I will be his Father, and he shall be My son.
If he commits iniquity, I will chasten him with the rod of men and with the blows of the sons of men.
But My mercy shall not depart from him, as I took it from Saul, whom I removed from before you.
And your house, your kingdom, your throne shall be established forever." [19]

David was known for being a shepherd, a musician, a warrior, and defeating the enemy giant Goliath.
Now You called David, "a man after Your own heart" and had Samuel anoint him to replace King Saul.
Now Saul was a Benjamite who failed to obey and the promised Messiah was to come from Judah.
Saul did not give up his kingship easily and hunted David to kill him and his growing company.
Through those seven long years when David could have killed Saul he refused to harm the LORD's anointed.

David was honorable in this and Saul, mortally wounded in battle by the Philistines, took his own life.
David then was first appointed king over Judah and reigned for seven and half years from Hebron.
Then he was anointed king over all of Israel and reigned for thirty-three more years in Jerusalem.
He had six wives in Hebron and married Bathsheba during his reign in Jerusalem.
Bathsheba, daughter of Eliam, a mighty Gilonite warrior of David, was a Canaanite too.

For David and Bathsheba this was not an honorable union for Bathsheba was married to Uriah.
David illicitly took Bathsheba in adultery and she conceived his son.
He tried to cover up her pregnancy by bringing Uriah home to bed his wife.
Uriah, one of David's mighty warriors, refused to sleep with her while his men were actively at war.
So, David had Uriah take a letter to his captain, Joab, to place him into a fierce battle and withdraw.

So, Uriah was intentionally killed by David who then married the pregnant Bathsheba.
The prophet Nathan confronted him and David repented.
As Your judgment against David, the infant boy dies before his eighth day of circumcision and naming.
You forgive David his sin with Bathsheba and Your Holy Spirit was not removed from him.
Now two of David's children born to Bathsheba, Solomon and Nathan, are in the lineage of Christ. [20]

Abba, we first see David as a humble shepherd who protects his father's sheep against a bear and a lion.
He is skilled with a slingshot, risking his life for the sheep, a skill that comes in handy with Goliath.
Christ comes as our Good Shepherd humbling Himself to come to mankind as an infant.
He is born to the virgin Mary through David's son, Nathan, and Joseph's lineage is traced to Solomon.
Jesus is born in Bethlehem at the Midgal Eder where sacrificial sheep are birthed as the prophets foretold.

David is the greatest king of Israel although not sinless,
He defeated the enemies of Israel and made the Israelites secure and prosperous.
Jesus will someday return to secure His beloved children.
His sacrifice on the cross means He conquered Satan, sin, and death for us.
If David foreshadows Christ, then David's Jerusalem foreshadows the new Jerusalem.

By lineage Jesus Christ is of the royal house of David by Mary and his adopted father Joseph.
Solomon's kingship was stable but his son Rehoboam lost his reign over ten of the tribes of Israel.
You, keeping Your promise to David, allows Rehoboam to hold on to the tribes of Judah and Benjamin.
In time, both the Northern and Southern tribes of Israel were destroyed and dispersed for idolatry.
Jesus our Messiah came to take kingship of the spiritual lives of His children while time runs to completion.

Jesus Christ, our perfect sinless substitute, fills all the more than three hundred prophecies of the Messiah.
As planned He came in the time of the Romans who used crucifixion as a means of death for non-Romans.
Although found innocent by the Roman governor, Pilate, of any Roman law, He is condemned to be crucified.
Under Jewish law, Jesus was guilty of blasphemy for confessing truthfully to being Your son.
Blasphemy was a stoning offense but Your plan of salvation had Jesus obedient to the cross.

Jesus, our Messiah, came to be Your light to a lost and dying world.
He came in the love of the Trinity for mankind to be their salvation and restoration.
He came to face a criminal's death for me so I would not have to face eternity separated from the You.
He came to be my substitute sacrifice to be crucified for me, the cruelest means of death.
He gave up His life for me and took it up again on Resurrection Sunday.

Our Savior, Jesus Christ, is the only one worthy of the eternal throne of David.
He will rule not only in the hearts of His beloved but from His throne.
When time is complete, the old heaven and earth will pass away.
The new heaven and earth will be established and we will live forever in glorified eternal bodies.
Heaven will come down to earth and Christ will rule from the Davidic throne as You promised.

The Davidic throne will then forever have a son of David ruling from it.
For that Son, the only Son of God, is the One and only truly Eternal King.
Abba, I remember the Holy Communion covenant Christ made the night before His death.
I remember my Savior's suffering, His body abused and tortured for me.
I remember His blood poured out for me, His full payment of my sin debt.

I was set free by my Jesus and I am free indeed.

Good Friday April 15, 2022

Now Abba, it is Friday night and Jesus' body is laying in Joseph's tomb but He is setting the captives free and claiming the keys to Hades and Death. And I know Sunday is coming and He arose that first Sunday after His crucifixion. I know too that many saints that had died before His crucifixion were resurrected with Him on Resurrection Sunday. This is amazing proof that Jesus conquered sin and death and that we are eternal beings. These saints were resurrected and seen by their loved ones. In His death, Jesus, set the righteous dead free of their sins, and offers this freedom to all who will follow after Him.

Abba, Sunday is now here and I celebrate the Resurrection of my Savior. He is risen! He is risen indeed. Thank you Abba, Holy Spirit and Jesus for the gift of salvation and restoration. Amen.

The Temple Veil and Saints Resurrected

The veil of the temple was the work of skilled artisans, Abba.
It was made as You directed Moses and You provided Moses with the materials and artisans.
The veil was beautiful, sixty feet high, thirty wide, and four inches thick.
It was made of fine twisted linen of blue, purple, and scarlet material.
Giant cherubim were embroidered into it and it served a special purpose.
This veil was Your protection for Your children as no one could enter the Holy of Holies and live.

The veil was the closed door between You and sinful man.
It was the division between the Holy Place where priests served daily and the Holy of Holies.
Only once a year, on the Day of Atonement, the High Priest for that year could enter there.
He had to atone for his sins before entering and then atone for sins of the people.
Only the blood of his animal sacrifice substitute could see him survive death and his duty that day.
Yet, as a failsafe a rope was tied around his waist in case he died so he could be dragged out.

The Holy of Holies represented Your presence, Abba.
The veil was a visual barrier between You and sinful man and its meaning was made quite clear to all.
Since the tabernacle had first been installed in the wilderness, the veil was present.
So, when Solomon built the elaborate temple in Jerusalem this uniquely crafted veil hung there.
Now priests in Aaron's line offered sacrifices daily at six, twelve, three, and six by Your law given to Moses.
So, on the day Jesus' crucifixion priests were in the Holy place and the veil was beautiful, unmarred, and whole.

Now on the day of the crucifixion of Christ, there was darkness over all the earth from noon to three o'clock. [1]
This strange darkness was a barrier as Your wrath came against Jesus who took on our sins.
This is the only recorded time and event where Jesus' fellowship with You and the Holy Spirit was lost.
So, Jesus was in great spiritual agony when he called out to You as God and not His Father,
"My God, My God, why have You forsaken Me?" [2]
Sin separates any of us from God, and in bearing our sin, Jesus experienced this tremendous loss.

Yet, He came to be our substitute sacrifice, to pay a debt we could not ever pay.
Then the sun was darkened, and the veil of the temple was torn in two. [3]
And Jesus cried out again with a loud voice and yielded up His spirit.
Then, behold, the veil of the temple was torn in two from top to bottom;
and the earth quaked, and the rocks were split. [4]
This was Your plan, the plan Jesus obeyed, Your plan of restoration from the foundation of the world.

After this, Jesus knowing that all things were now accomplished,
that the Scripture might be fulfilled, said, **"I thirst!"** *And Jesus was given sour wine and said,*
"It is finished!" *And bowing His head, He gave up His spirit.* [5]
"It is finished" in Greek word *tetelestai*, is an accounting term, which means paid in full.
Jesus was saying that the debt I owed You for my sin as a daughter of Adam was fully satisfied .
The plan of salvation and restoration made at the creation of the world was now complete.

Then Luke tells us, *"And when Jesus had cried out with a loud voice, He said,*
"Father, into Your hands I commit My spirit. " *Having said this, He breathed His last.* [6]
This was not Jesus succumbing to His brutal injuries, blood loss, dehydration, and shock.
This is Jesus, in a unique act of power, voluntarily giving up His life.
The dying thieves are still alive but Jesus fulfilling all the prophecies of the Messiah breathes His last.
Now John was at the cross of Jesus when He died and Luke wrote from eyewitness accounts.

Both accounts of these last words of Jesus are tremendously significant.
John records that man's sin debt was paid and Jesus felt His fellowship with His Father was restored.
As our sinless divine Savior, He called out to His Father, our Father, to receive His Spirit.
Jesus didn't die with a whimper but gave the clear victory shout, **"It is finished!"** [7]
Abba, Jesus had been commissioned by You to come, teach, heal, and die as the final sacrifice for mankind.
This ended His earthly life of obedience, humility, and suffering that sets anyone free who will ask.

The tearing of the veil in two at the time of Jesus' death was of great import.
Jesus' death was the ultimate blood sacrifice that opened a new and living way into the presence of God.
Since Jesus offered Himself up as the final perfect sacrifice, four daily sacrifices were no longer needed.
This purpose of the physical Temple in Jerusalem and animal sacrifices ended.
Sinful man no longer needed to be physically separated from You for Jesus had opened a way to You.
It clearly showed that the Jewish religious system had ended and that Jesus was now our high priest.

But when Christ appeared as a high priest of the good things that had come,
through the greater and more perfect temple, Himself, not made with hands of this creation.
He entered once for all into the most Holy of Holies, not by means of the blood of goats and calves.
He entered by means of His own blood, thus securing an eternal redemption. [8]
So, then it is only Christ who can cleanse our consciences from dead works to serve You our living God! [9]
Jesus said, "I am the way, the truth, and the life. No one comes to the Father except through Me." [10]

Jesus was our true Passover Lamb dying on the afternoon of Passover.
His death was at the time when the Jews in Jerusalem were preparing their lambs for Passover.
And because He was the true Passover lamb, You did not allow a bone in His body to be broken.
Under Mosaic law the Passover lambs bones could not be broken and this was a prophecy too of the Messiah.
"They shall leave none of the lamb until morning, nor break one of its bones.
According to all the ordinances of the Passover they shall keep the lamb." [11]

"Now it was the day of Preparation for the Passover Sabbath.
The Jewish leaders did not want the men's bodies left on their crosses during the Sabbath.
*So, they asked Pilate to have their legs **broken** and their bodies taken down.*
The soldiers therefore came and broke the legs of the men crucified with Jesus.
But when they came to Jesus and found that He was already dead, they did not break His legs.
Instead, one of the soldiers pierced Jesus' side with a spear, bringing a sudden flow of blood and water." [12]

David in a Psalms one-thousand years before Christ crucifixion says,
"You, Abba, guard all His bones; and not one of them is broken. [13]
So, not only is the prophecy that Jesus bones would not be broken fulfilled but so is this one about piercing.
And again, another Scripture says, "They shall look on Him whom they pierced." [14]
"And finally, Behold, He is coming with clouds, and every eye will see Him, even those who pierced Him.
And all the tribes of the earth will mourn because of Him. Even so, Amen." [15]

Abba, let me look at Golgotha Hill one more time at the non-believers there.
To the hardened Gentile Roman centurions this was just another crucifixion.
But Matthew said, *"When the centurion and those with him, those guarding Jesus,*
Saw the earthquake and the things that had happened,
They feared greatly, saying, 'Truly this was the Son of God!' [16]
Yes, they were justly afraid, Abba, but did they become the first among the saved after Christ's crucifixion?

Abba, when Jesus was a newborn He was taken to the temple where Simeon blessed them.
Simeon said to Mary His mother, "Behold, this Child is destined for the fall and rising of many in Israel,
And for a sign which will be spoken against, a sword will pierce through your own soul also,
That the thoughts of many hearts may be revealed." [17]
Simeon's prophecy came true too, Abba, for Mary was at her son and Savior's crucifixion.
She saw as His mother and a sinner, Jesus' great suffering and only understood He died until Sunday came.

I repeat this scripture now, Abba, turning away from the renting of the veil.
I want to look at the resurrection scripture.
"And Jesus cried out again with a loud voice and yielded up His spirit.
Then, behold, the veil of the temple was torn in two from top to bottom; and the earth quaked,
and the rocks were split, and the graves of many saints who had fallen asleep were raised;
and coming out of the graves after His resurrection, they went into the holy city and appeared to many." [18]

Ah, Abba, I pause to reflect.
The resurrection of saints is not an event of Jesus' crucifixion and resurrection often mentioned.
Perhaps because such an event can't be explained and scripture tells us no details.
These saints were raised from their graves on Friday at the time Jesus surrendered His spirit to You.
Then after Jesus' resurrection at the dawn of Sunday they went into the holy city and were seen.
No, we don't know who they are; how many, and what they did between Friday night and Sunday morning.

We don't know how long they stayed or lived in their resurrected form.
We don't if they died again or if they were supernaturally taken into heaven.
We do know they were saints, believers, that had died before Your son was crucified for them.
We know they were asleep in You and raised from among the dead.
We know on that resurrection morning of Your son they went into the city of Jerusalem.
We know there were many eyewitnesses to their resurrection but don't know how they reacted or believed.

We can list six miracles of Jesus Christ's crucifixion and resurrection.
There was darkness at midday and the temple veil which was rented in two from top to bottom.
There was a local earthquake which split large rocks but did not damage any buildings in nearby Jerusalem.
The earthquake opened the graves of saints in the vicinity of the cross of Christ at the time of Christ's death.
Christ's guarded empty tomb had His wrapping left intact and His face cloth was left neatly folded nearby.
How is it we don't wonder at number six; the saints being supernaturally resurrected with Him?

Surely, this was dramatic proof that Jesus had triumphed over death itself.
"But now Christ is risen from the dead and has become the firstfruits of those who have fallen asleep.
For since by man came death, by Man also came the resurrection of the dead.
For as in Adam all die, even so in Christ all shall be made alive." [19]
It is proof that these believers did not die foolishly trusting in eternal life.
It is all the proof I need to know that we are eternal beings whose eternal spirit lives forever.

Although I am surprised that not more is spoken of the resurrection of the saints when Christ died,
Abba, I like that John, Jesus' beloved disciple said: *"Do not marvel at this;*
For the hour is coming in which all who are in the graves will hear His voice
And come forth—those who have done good, to the resurrection of life,
And those who have done evil, to the resurrection of condemnation." [20]
John knew Christ, was granted the power to do miracles; suffered for Him and died; and believed in eternal life.

But wait, not just the good to the resurrection of life, but the evil to the resurrection of eternal suffering.
So, mankind, eternal beings all, face judgment for their accepting or rejecting Christ and the plan of salvation.
You, Abba, want no one to spend eternity separated from You in a place of eternal condemnation.
This is why Jesus was the lamb worthy to be slain for mankind from the foundation of the world.
Jesus obediently paid for the plan of restoration and salvation with His own death on Calvary.
So, every immortal soul must choose eternal life in heaven with You or eternal life separated from You.

The Apostle Paul in agreement with John said this in his letter to the church in Rome.
God *"will render to each one according to his deeds":*
eternal life to those who by patient continuance in doing good seek
For glory, honor, and immortality; but to those who are self-seeking and do not obey the truth,
But obey unrighteousness—indignation and wrath, tribulation and anguish,
On every soul of man who does evil," without partiality. [21]

We are indeed eternal beings. Did Jesus not raise Lazarus from the dead after he was four days in his grave?
Yes, remember too beloved that the dying thief went to Paradise to be with our Savior that day.
These raised saints went into Jerusalem as witnesses to Jesus' victory over the power of sin and death.
I imagine there were priests who not only saw the renting of the veil but visited with some of these saints.
Yes, I imagine there were sincere priests who had been waiting for the Messiah to come who had seen death.
Imagine being a priest that weekend, seeing the veil eerily split and having a visit with someone long dead.

John tells us that many believed in Jesus but did not all follow after Him before or after His crucifixion.
Within their freewill, they favored their way of life over pursuing Jesus. A mistake we should avoid.
Nevertheless, even among the rulers many believed in Him, but because of the
Pharisees they did not confess Him, lest they should be put out of the synagogue;
For they loved the praise of men more than the praise of God. [22]
Sadly, they chose the temporary things of this world (condemnation) over eternal life in Christ.

By our own freewill, as eternal beings, we have a choice of where we spend the eternal days of our lives.
We can elect Your plan of salvation and restoration which Jesus' sacrificial crucifixion bought.
Or we can choose eternal separation from You and Paradise as did the unrepentant thief.
Now, Abba, as a mortal being knowing my earthly body will fail, it is hard to imagine eternal days without end.
But then I don't even want to imagine days of eternal suffering apart from You with no hope of a second chance.
So, putting aside imagining I am just going to rely on my faith that You supply through Your grace and mercy.

Forever and always. Amen. Easter 2022

Abba, this is my third Easter piece that came about from our ELL Bible Study, that I gave over Matthew 27:50-53. I never saw before that the saints raised on Friday when Jesus died, were not resurrected until Resurrection Sunday. Praise Abba. I liked Dave Early's sermon today too. (4/24) He asked, "What will Matter 1,000 years from now." I asked that of my two teen nephews in a written prayer poem for them today. Please restore them, Abba, my soul needs to share eternity with them. Thank you, LORD Jesus, Your world without end. Amen.

Chapter Two

Christmas Offerings

It was long my privilege to take Good Friday off from work and anticipate what the Holy Spirit would have for me. Then the Holy Spirit began to speak to me with Christmas offerings. God's chosen used to offer sacrifices as an atonement for their sins before Christ died as the final atonement that was wholly acceptable to God. But all their sacrifices came from what God had supplied to them. These pieces are supplied to me. My sacrifice, if you would, is my time, and even it comes from the Father. It is hard to explain the beauty and joy that comes from these pieces and how God is growing me. They are truly food for my soul and fire shut up in my bones. A fire that on these pages I can share and hope will ignite a fire in you. This intimacy with God is a great gift and a treasure beyond value.

Snowmen

Snowmen are unrecognized ambassadors of God and His love.
They are made of water, yet they are not clear.
Snowmen appear in limited places, for limited times, after special weather conditions,
But must be created by joyful hands.
The crystalline flakes used to bring them to life cannot be counted,
And no two flakes are alike.
They are made in child-like joy, and they can be clothed,
And like us they all have their own characteristics.

Snowmen are unrecognized ambassadors of God and His love, because
God gave us water and we are all creations of His hands.
His love for us cannot be counted and none of us are alike,
Not even those called identical for our souls are uniquely our own.
God gave us the gift of childlikeness and He enjoys seeing us use this gift.
And He allows all of us to develop our own characteristics,
But He would prefer that we take on His own characteristics.

God is love and God loves us and His love for us will never end or melt away.

Christmas 2001

Father, I think this piece shows You have a sense of humor and whimsy. We often don't think of the softer characteristics of ours that came from You. We were made, Father, in Your image. So, thank you for reminding me that You are our tender Father who seeks to delight Himself in us, so You did not make us robots. Thank you that Your love is forever, and Your kingdom, power, and glory know no end. I count, Father, too, on Your grace and mercy that comes new every morning. My love, Father. Amen.

Wise Men

Wise men sought Him because they understood
The prophecies concerning His birth.
Their journey to Him was long and arduous
and they suffered the perils of crossing mountains, rivers, deserts
And plains where they dealt with strange people of
Other cultures and languages.

Their travel filled weeks, months, and years and yet
They journeyed on without map or guidepost.
But, because they sought God's promised Messiah,
God provided them with a star on which to chart their course.
A new star spun into the night sky to announce Christ's obedience,
A star no doubt woven from the glory shared by Father and Son.

Love was the first element of God's great gift to man.
God, Christ, and the Holy Spirit's love reaching out to us.
The second gift was Jesus giving up Heaven for His human lifetime.
Yes, Jesus gave up this intimate relationship with the Father and Holy Spirit.
Obedience was the third element that paved the way for our
Restoration to the Trinity.

The angel, Gabrielle, came to announce God's plan of salvation to the Virgin called Mary
And she accepted His proclamation and became the vessel that carried Christ.
Then, Joseph, a worthy and honorable man had revealed to him in a dream God's plan
And took Mary to be his wife and Christ to be his firstborn son.
They were obedient to God's call and obedience was
Not the easy choice, but their choice.

By obeying man's law, they traveled when Mary was great
With the child to Joseph's birthplace to be counted for a tax.
And so, the taxing was the simple earthly reason
That brought about the fulfillment
Of the prophecy that Christ's birth would be in Bethlehem
Because He was a descendent of the royal house of King David.

Humbly then Christ's great essence came in obedience
To a cruel dark world to be its peace, hope, and light.
After Mary gave birth to Christ,
She wrapped Him in swaddling clothes,
Laid Him in a manger to watch over Him
And ponder the events of His birth in her heart.

Imagine the night sky as it broke open and the angels
Came in their heavenly raiment to raise the anthem of praise and worship,
To make the announcement of Christ the Savior's birth to a lost world,
To lowly despised shepherds keeping watch over their flocks.
The shepherds had no gifts to offer, and none were asked or needed that night,
Because the ultimate gift was God's beloved son, Jesus Christ.

The religious leaders knew of the prophecies of Christ's birth, and ignored them
Out of fear until the wise men from the East came bearing gifts to the newborn king.
These wise men came to the King's palace expecting to find
The King of Kings living in earthly splendor.
But Christ did not come to earth to live in earthly splendor,
But to dwell in the hearts of men and women, to live as they lived.

The political leaders of the day plotted and sent the wise men on
In their journey to find the place where Christ lived with Mary and Joseph.
They said, "Go and find Him, return to us, and we too will go to worship Him."
Religious leaders and earthly rulers alike could not be bothered to go with them,
But the wise men did not lose heart at this setback in their quest,
But continued their journey until they found the young child.

Those wise men and all those traveling with them started a journey to Christ,
Stayed the course through difficulties until they at last found Him.
Then, they fell down and worshiped the Christ child and gave Him gifts that were used
In His journey to manhood and the cross of Calvary. Gold because He was born a King
That would rule our hearts and lives. Frankincense because He was born to become our high priest.
And myrrh because He was in death to become our ultimate sacrifice.

Then, being warned by God in a dream they started their journey home another way,
Bypassing the courts of the King and religious leaders alike
Who would have attempted to kill Christ and God's plan of redemption.
They came seeking and brought gifts,
And not doubt left with the gift of their eternal lives in the heavenlies,
Because no man can stand in the presence of God and walk away unchanged.

Obedience brought Christ to earth to dwell among us.
Obedience gave Him earthly parents to shepherd His growth.
Obedience took wise men home another route to protect the young child and His parents.
Obedience saw Christ grow strong in His earthly relationship to His Heavenly Father.
Obedience saw Him through His wilderness temptation.
Obedience saw Christ take our place on the cross and saw Him rise again the third day.

Obedience is the only cost of being a child of God.
Adam and Eve failed to obey and lost their unique relationship to God
And their disobedience is our birthright. God through unconditional love planned to restore
Us to Himself and Christ's love and obedience paid the price of our restoration.
All we must do in obedience is accept the gift of salvation offered to us
That was bought at a great price with Christ's sacrifice.

It's all there for the taking even the grace to accept the gift that
We are not worthy to have by our own work or merit.
Unconditional love is offered and all we have to do is take it,
Allow Christ to live through us while we sojourn here on earth,
And then spend eternity with Him where there is no want, or sorrow,
Only joy, at last the "happy ever after" we all desire to find.

Amen
December 15, 2002

Father, this piece is so different from the one You gave me last year. It is profoundly serious, and I like it because it came through me. It is a gift that I share with You every time I read it. We all want what was our garden legacy lost through disobedience. Thank you for Your plan to restore us to Your original plan. Teach us obedience so we don't fail to obey; teach us to listen for Your call; and teach us to act according to Your will. Then, Father forgive us yet again when we fail, pick us up, dust us off, kiss our wounds, and give us the courage to try once again. Sin isn't what we want for ourselves, so show us how to follow hard after You, so we do not disappoint, but delight You. All glory, honor, and praise, Father, Jesus, and Holy Spirit. Amen.

Legend of the First Snow Woman

When the world was yet still new,
God looked at his vast creation and was pleased.

His gaze caught momentarily the high mountains where the snow
Laid undisturbed sparkling like diamonds.

There God stretched out His hand and lifted up a measure of snow.
His breath touched the fresh snow, and in a twinkle, He held the first Snow Woman.

He sat her gently upon a plain in her new home,
And she bowed down to worship Him.

Their relationship was established that first moment,
The Father and His beloved child.
Time passed and they fellowshipped each day,
Snow Woman remained content with little to say.

God came one day, saddened because of the incident in the garden,
**He spoke with her, "I offer you a choice. I will give you a companion,
So that you will no longer be alone. You may have a spouse, a child, or a friend."**

Snow Woman replied, "All these years I have never been alone,
For I have always had You to call upon. I have called You friend
And more I have called You Father."

**"The world is changing snowwoman, so,
I will bless you for your steadfastness."**

"As Your child, I have always had Your unconditional love.
If I must choose, give me a child,
So, I can love him with the same unconditional love and favor You have given me.
For I will teach him of Your mercies, and he will love You as I do."

God was pleased with the wisdom of her choice.
**"In as much as you have placed our relationship above all else,
I will give you not only a child, but a spouse, and a friend."
Then, He warned her. "They may prove to be burdensome."**

A single tear rolled down Snow Woman's cold cheek,
And with an outstretched finger God took the tear
And warmed her heart. "If those You give me become
burdensome, I will give You praise, because just as You took
My tear and comforted my heart, so will You take the burden
They might place on me. And I will gratefully allow You
To carry the burden as You have always cherished and carried me."

God looked at His creation, His child and was pleased,
With her child-like heart and her understanding of their relationship.
Then He called to the heavens and the clouds opened wide
To reveal Jesus Christ, God's only Son.

"The plan will go forward." Jesus acknowledged and the
Angels began to sing Hosanna.
"Yes, the Father replied. "Mankind needs a Savior."
Christ bowed His head in obedience and the Father was pleased with His son.

2003

Abba, this is my second poem about snowmen or more in this case a snowwoman. Although the poem is very spiritual and deep, it touches me because the character is not human. In this little piece, she did what we as humans could not do. She was faithful, steadfast, and grateful. This poem came through the Holy Spirit to remind me of the relationship we all should seek with You. It reminds me that the world was once without sin and Jesus, after sin came to Eden, gave up Heaven to become my Savior. There is a unique beauty in this poem because of its symbolism and realism. I pray that You will continue to find reasons to delight in me, to guide, to teach me, rebuke and forgive me, until I stand before You throne not in judgment but in Christ's love for me. Abba thank you for all of creation and its restoration someday where I will enjoy it in the Eternal with all Your children gathered Home. Amen.

Christmas is Still Christmas

Christmas is heralded as the biggest holiday event of the year.
Retailers anticipate and pin their hopes on high revenues
And stress over bad economic times and poor sales.
Adults bemoan the expense of the holiday, and despite parties
And receiving gifts they can't wait for the season to pass.

Indeed, many suffer from depression and suicide rates increase.
Small children are taught to wait all year for Santa Claus,
A fictional character who magically delivers toys
Worldwide to *good* children in just one night.
Older children cut to the chase and just present their wish lists.

Christmas is not an annual holiday,
But truly the remembrance of the Event.
Christ left the splendor of heaven and came to our
World that laid in endless darkness and sin.
He came in obedience to the plan of our salvation that He knew
Would end in His torment, humiliation, torture, and cruel death,
He came to us a mere babe to lowly earthly parents.

Angels announced His birth.
Shepherds, the despised and rejected workers
Of their time were invited by angels to witness His coming.
Wise men from the East traveled to bring Him gifts and failing
To find Him in the expected location, Herod's palace,
Found him in a humble dwelling where they opened their kingly gifts
Of frankincense, gold, and myrrh to Him as a young child.

Then, being warned of Herod's intended evil in a dream,
They returned to their county without divulging the Christ child's location.
Seldom included in Christ's birth story, Herod, Esau's descendant then killed
All the male children two years and younger in all of Bethlehem
And the surrounding area in an effort to destroy Christ.
Jesus was a perceived threat to his earthly throne, but the true threat to Satan.
This great evil did not touch Christ, nor alter the plan of redemption.

Satan could not destroy Christ as a child or tempt Him to sin as an adult.
Could do nothing to change the plan of redemptive love that Christ
Bought with His humble birth, earthly ministry, betrayal, torture,
Crucifixion, burial, and victorious resurrection.

But Satan's evil is patient and with each passing Christmas the world
Steps further away from the true meaning of Christmas.
How sad that in our country that was founded because
A few sought religious freedom that Christmas is no longer politically correct.

Christmas has been merged with other holidays celebrated this time of year,
And so, we are supposed to wish relatives and friends
"Happy Holidays" or "Season Greetings."
We are told that since all do not believe in Christ and Christmas,
That we should respect their disbelief by hiding our own – how foolish.
Celebrating Christmas has not yet been forbidden for
This season of holiday decorating, partying, and gift giving is
Profitable and greed is an evil that still feeds.

Christianity, Christ centered religion, still lives
In our county, my faith remains strong.
So, do not ask me to forgo my faith for political correctness.
I remind you that political correctness allows all to believe as
They choose and therefore cannot preclude Christianity.
I remind all to allow my freedoms that so many have died to protect.
Those freedoms that still include the freedom to speak,
To assemble, and the freedom of religious choice.

One of my favorite praise choruses symbolizes Christ's
betrayal and death as " A rose trampled on the ground."
My heart sees a beautiful freshly cut red rose
Tossed on the ground where careless feet walk over it.
I come upon it and carefully pick it up,
Shelter it from further harm and take it home
And place it in a bud vase of water in a place of honor.
I look at it occasionally as I pass.
Then, night gives way to day, darkness to light
And the damaged petals that once clung perilously
To the stem are now whole and rigidly attached.

The Christ of Christmas remains unchanged
By centuries of efforts to dethrone Him.
In my heart, I replay His life from the glory He shared
with the Father before His birth to His ascension back to Heaven.
It includes the angel's visit to His virgin mother Mary
And Joseph's instructions though dreams.
It amazes me that Mary and Joseph were from the royal house of King David.

I see His birth at the Tower of Migdal Eder
And the visits of the nearby shepherds,
And the gifts of the long-suffering wise men.
I remember the story of His youth where He stayed behind to teach in Jerusalem.
And I glory in His ministry among us, His teachings, His miracles, His betrayal,
His death, and His glorious resurrection – all done for me.

King Jesus lives and is my intercessor with the Father in His throne room.
The story of Christmas can't exclude Christ for me for without Christ
There is no Christmas. I cannot exclude Christ from my life,
Because without Him I am **void**. He took my darkness and replaced
It with the light of His amazing eternal love. So, I've said all this
From my heart, to remind us to think of all this Event means.
To tell you it is right to believe, and to summarize it with just this,
"Merry Christmas."

2008

Father, Your Son Jesus, was the long-awaited heir to the throne of His earthly parents, King David. His coming literally fulfilled over three-hundred prophecies about the coming Messiah, yet there are those who don't believe Jesus is the One. Thank you, I believe. My heart understands all that my mind can't find the words to say or to share. So, Holy Spirit, speak for me and share the truth so that all may believe in Christ Jesus our Returning King. To You Father, Savior Jesus, and Holy Spirit glory and praise forever. Amen.

They Can't Take Jesus Away!

"The attack has been insidious, clever, and has taken centuries.
"Operation Discredit Jesus" is winding down and victory is within my grasp."
Satan faintly glowed with pleasure as he closed his right hand in a tight fist to emphasize his statement.
And the attending demons cheered and murmured to each other in joyful agreement.
"We have taken Jesus away."

"The witnesses to the Holy Birth and the farce of His death are centuries dead
And the ancestors of the witnesses don't even know who they are."
Satan snickered, "So, there is no one to share or confirm the truth to the coming generations."
The demons danced in unholy delight.

Perversion roared in a deep belly laugh. "Yes, it has taken time,
But the religious reviewers no longer believe in the virgin birth.
The word of Isaiah that spoke of the virgin giving birth is now being translated
As a young woman or better, young married woman.
And the gospel accounts of Mary the virgin mother are being discounted,
Although the word can only be translated as virgin."

One of the lesser demons of Distraction chortled in agreement.
"Yes, yes, these modern individuals are so intelligent and so sophisticated,"
he spoke in a falsetto, "and so busy that it has been easy to distract them from the truth."
Satan agreed. "Ah, the truth of the lowly birth has indeed been diluted by time
And the stories of angels announcing the birth, shepherds and wise men coming
Are just a part of the Christian myth."

Mayhem wanted his due, so he strutted forward and raised his hands to gain attention.
"Look at all we've accomplished by moving the people from what is holy
To focusing on shopping, decorating, partying, and, oh yes,
The focus on more and more presents – more things.
One of the greatest holidays of the year that once was celebrated quietly with reflection
On everything holy is now the holiday of More, More, More, not Him!"

Discord pulled Mayhem aside to gain attention.
"And look what we have accomplished with political correctness,
neutrality, and respect for all teachings. It is no longer Merry Christmas and Happy New Year,
But Happy Holidays and all the religious symbols of this High Holy Day,
Are commercially sold for the dollar, but practically banished from acceptability
So as not to offend someone of a non-Christian faith."

Mayhem pushed Discord aside, none too gently, and spoke.
"Yes, you all have done well, but what of all those other religions?
"Born a Jew, many modern Jews still reject Jesus as their Messiah,
And still wait for His promised first appearance."

He nodded in self-satisfaction and grinned.
"Look how we handled Abraham's sons, Isaac and Ishmael.
There is no greater record of brotherly discord that has borne such fruit. Why –."
Hate broke in, "Yes, look how far we have fanned their animosity."
The two brothers have become multiple cultures filled with hate for each other and –"

"Look what you have done?!!" Terror roared.
"We have made the world a troubled and unsafe place
for all and the Americans who felt so safe." He chortled in contempt,
"Well not one of them will forget 911.
He grinned and struck his chest in self-glorification.
"Terror doesn't even have to be real now, but only imagined and they have
Whole agencies running rampant over their freedoms looking for hidden terrorists."

There was movement in the back of the room that caught Satan's eye,
"Doubt where are you going? What about your report?
Your brothers have done well and certainly your service has always been valued."
Doubt turned to his master and swallowed hard and kept his place near the opened door.
He did not want to breathe any doubt into this meeting.

"Indeed, master we serve. In times of darkness we strike,
And make the people doubt their salvation;
Doubt their Savior's love and even His existence.
A little doubt in a human's mind goes a long way and these modern times
Have made it so much easier for our brothers of Distraction to keep them
Busy with high-speed everything. They can now rely on themselves,
Medicine and" he laughed bitterly, *"the internet at their fingertips."*

"Yes, modern man no longer needs a great big God
To take care of their petty ordinary needs." Satan roared with laughter
And the demons save Doubt joined him. "They no longer need to pray for their daily bread,
But select their gourmet coffee and swipe their cards."

Doubt hung his head, **"Indeed Master it is as you have planned.**
The world needs a Savior who has already come, but many cannot feel the need of Him,
See His hand of mercy or realize His abundant unconditional love for them."

Satan paused reflectively as the demons surrounding him roared their approval and satisfaction.
"Why are you troubled then Doubt?"

"We are in the churches, Master."

"Yes, you have been highly successful there.
Churches have closed for lack of attendance. Other churches preach brotherly love,
Feel good messages, and many discount the Bible, or leave it out altogether."

"Indeed Master, there are those, but the others preach the word as it is written."

"These few trouble you, Doubt?" Satan asked as his eyes pierced and held the demon's.

"My Lord, they do for they are not so few, and they send out their kind
To preach the truth to those who have not heard it."
Doubt swallowed again hard and looked to the door.

"But the old guard is dying out." Satan encouraged.

"Master, this is true, but they are being replaced with a new generation and Revelation says, –."

"Revelation!" Satan roared, and Doubt shrank from his wrath. "You know the book?"

"Master, don't be angry with your humble servants.
We go to church to stir doubt amongst the believers, and the book is being read.
We hear the words and whisper that it is too hard to appreciate,
Too symbolic to understand, that it is better left unopened,
But to those who believe it doesn't have to be clear for them to understand."

"What manner of nonsense then do you speak, Doubt?" Satan eyed him.
"It is full of symbolism, and hard for man to understand,
And there are multiple interpretations as so many other things in the Bible.
How do they understand?"

Doubt wished himself away and hated what he must report.
He was the lead Demon of Doubt after all.
"They don't have to understand all that is written to understand that their Savior,
Jesus Christ came and paid the price of their sins.
That He is their advocate at the right hand of the Father, and that
He has promised that even to the end of the world that they cannot be snatched from His hand."

Satan roared at these words and his displeasure,
Causing the demons standing nearby to push back,
Many covered their ears. Others ran to the door as Doubt continued.

"They understand that no matter when the end,
Or how, they win eternity with heaven coming to a renewed earth."
Doubt laughed in a dry mirth and finished, **"and we will be cast into a lake of fire**
With all the unsaved souls who have believed our lies."

2011

Father, there are those who don't believe that Satan and his followers, demons, are real, so they certainly don't believe they are in our world working against human souls to deceive them and draw them into the eternal lake of fire prepared for the demons and the destination of deceived souls. Now I have read the Bible and know that Satan and demons are our adversaries, and I know they have no power over the saved but that they still want to steal our joy and rob us of our testimony and praise of the Trinity living and working for all the beloved. Yet, free choice, this wonderful gift of freewill You designed into man means I can't convince or argue anyone into believing the message of the free gift of salvation. Please continue, Holy Spirit, to strive with the spirit of men and women and present the truth to them. Continue to rebuke Satan and his demons from interfering with anyone who will come to salvation and with all the saved. Your beloved daughter prays Your will in this, for I know it is Your will for all to be saved. Eternal praise now and forevermore. Your world without end Holy Father. Amen.

Rhoda's Song of Praise

You made me in the image of the Trinity.
I was made in Your likeness, Father— body, mind, and soul.
I was handmade to reflect You for eternity out of Triune Love.

My soul bends my body and mind to worship my Eternal Creator.
I bow at the feet of Father God, the Holy Spirit, and my sweet Savior Jesus.
The Holy Spirit moves through me and praise flows *to* my lips.

All that is within me must speak praises to the Divine.
My eternal soul knows no other Creator, Savior, and Comforter.
You breathed Your own breath into me to give me life. So, I worship You.

My lips cannot be silent for Jesus is my all and His glory fills me.
My heart sings angel songs for You the Great I Am.
Hear Father the words my mind and tongue *cannot* form.

Many of my family who are with you bore testimony to Your love.
Ever trusting they gave their lives to You and stood fast in faith.
My love story echoes theirs and builds upon their trust of You.

Your great grace and mercy were extended to my people.
They honored You and instructed their children the same.
You kept them in the hollow of Your outstretched hand.

My life touched another and a new generation came.
We lived our lives through You as a testimony to lead them to the Eternal.
They are now parents teaching their children Your mighty deeds.

Those You redeemed in the past now live still in eternity with You.
Those living now in You follow the path to heaven with You ever at their side.
Grant now this covenant to all who choose this great legacy—this gift of eternal love.

You brought down rulers with a tiny infant boy.
Through Jesus our coming King You built a bridge to heaven.
You lift up the humble in their time of need and give them food and rest.

My soul finds peace in this dark and troubled life.
You spoke the universe into being and gave me Your own breath.
When I breathe my last breath here, I will take my first eternal breath.

Jesus covered my debt and set this captive free.
I live in Him in a world restrained that only offers death.
Yet, I cannot be lost for my destiny lies with You beyond the stars.

I bow down this Christmas but my spirit soars to heaven.
There at heaven's throne I silently lay joyful tears at Your feet.
Your throne room is full, and time is nearly complete.

One day, joined to my glorified body my mind and soul will praise You near.
I will lift-up my eyes to see my Redeemer at Your right hand.
His eyes will look into mine with steadfast love and He will raise me up.

I will hear Jesus say, "She is one of ours, Father. I have gathered her to Me."
Then I will lift my voice in eternal song with all the throng.
"The Good Shepherd rescued us and is now and forever our Eternal King."

My soul bends the body and mind to worship the Eternal Creator.
I bow at the feet of Father God, the Holy Spirit, and my sweet Savior.
The Holy Spirit moves through me and praise flows *through* my lips.

Father, I wish that my mind could find the words to write how I feel about my relationship with You. Now I glory in You at a distance and my mind cannot fathom but hopes in that future where what is now restrained will be restored —earth, sky, and water. Nature will be at peace, and I will share time with You in the Eternal. Thank you for teaching me now, giving me a glimpse of heaven, and preparing my place there. Certainly, my spirit seems so small here, but knows that someday it will soar leaving behind the temporary for the permanent. May the Holy Spirit speak all praise to You my coming King. By Jesus' love and by His suffering, I am restored. Amen.

Have a Christ Blessed Christmas, 2016

King Jesus, Abide in Him

Before the universe was created, Jesus was **I AM**.
Three in one, The Trinity, with perfect unity was He.
Yet, He stepped away from His Heavenly throne to be God and Man.
King Jesus came as a babe in the royal line of King David He.

Time waned but David's kingdom was not lost although no son held his throne.
Mary, a virgin, was chosen to conceive Christ through the third member of the Trinity.
And as the prophets foretold, Mary delivered Him in David 's city, Bethlehem.
Oh, yes, King Jesus was born in the Migdal Eder, tower of the flock, as Micah foretold. [1]

Joseph was appointed Jesus' earthly father, and he was of royal blood.
Joseph was David's son through King Solomon.
Mary was David's daughter through his son, Nathan.
Since Mary and Joseph were royal descendants, they were chosen to parent King Jesus.

Oh, how far the royal line had fallen from prestige and pomp.
King Jesus, Savior of the world, had come to abide with them.
Mary and Joseph were chosen to rear Jesus to His earthly ministry.
Yet, He came to save them and us from sin and restore fellowship with **I AM**.

His parents were with Him twenty-four seven and He did abide with them.
Oh, yes, dear friend, they had a very personal relationship with Jesus.
Through our first parents, Adam and Eve, we were alienated from the Trinity.
Now, through Jesus, the Trinity had come to abide with them and us.

King Jesus was not a conquering earthy king.
He was humble and rode on a donkey for His triumphant ride into Jerusalem.
The people He had loved and ministered to strewed palm branches on His path.
Their greeting was "Hosanna" meaning rescue, save, savior.

I AM came to save us, indeed, to be our Savior.
The price was His very life for ours.
In just a few days, "Hosana" became "Crucify Him."
So, King Jesus was beaten, humiliated, spit upon, and struggled to climb Golgotha Hill.

There, King Jesus stretched out His arms and legs and was nailed to our cross.
He allowed Himself to be crucified as the final sacrifice for mankind's sin.
He gave up His life speaking to the Father and Spirit and us saying, "It is finished." [2]
Jesus' body, the lamb of God, was laid in a borrowed tomb and His followers mourned.

Oh, but Jesus was not finished, just the required sacrifice satisfied.
Jesus raised through His grave wrappings and laid his face napkin neatly aside.
Then, His followers saw Him alive and understood His teachings to them.
He commissioned them to "Go and Tell," even as they watched Him ascend to His throne in Heaven. [3]

So, dear friend, King Jesus' birth is why we celebrate this season.
Without His birth, Mary and Joseph would have been unknowns.
No, there would be no Christmas without the Christ of Christmas.
There would be no salvation if King Jesus hadn't come, ministered, and died.

Christmas is not the commercial holiday we celebrate.
It is the coming as foretold of King Jesus and His sacrifice.
Christmas would be all "Hosanna" without "Crucify Him."
His obedience to the cross provides our means of restoration to God.

King Jesus, please hear my praise and delight in my worship.
The napkin laid neatly aside means You are returning.
Many generations passed between King David and You.
But we bear witness that all foretold was true.

You came from King David to save us and restore us to Yourselves.
You are coming again to take up the earthly throne of David.
We are Your beloved children, and we worship You.
You are our hope of peace with God here on earth and throughout Eternity.

Father, I see and hear His anguish and know He was forsaken, not for anything He had done but because He took on the burden of my sin, all sin, for which mankind could not pay. He paid on that day the entire debt of sin; finished it on that day on the cross for me; and I am ever indebted and grateful because, I at my request, had His payment applied to my sin debt account. My account, marked paid in full, will come with a white robe of righteousness that Jesus paid so that I can stand in front of You and be welcomed forever home. Thank you, LORD, for giving us the gift of restoration and abiding with us here below and throughout Eternity. Abba, Son, and Holy Spirit, search us, I pray, and find reason to delight in us. Amen.

Christmas
December 21, 2019

Eternal Covenant Keeper

Abba, before You created the world, the Trinity shared agape love.
This agape love was so great that You wanted to share it, so You created mankind.
First, a place to amaze him – the ever-expanding universe with its wonders.
Then, a planet, Earth, to fill and a garden, Eden, for his home. [1]
There was unity between man, Adam, the creatures, and You, but man had no helpmate.

So, You took a rib from Adam's side and crafted Eve, a woman to share eternal life beside him.
Adam, You created from dust but woman from his rib and made them each a <u>living soul.</u> [2]
Unique creations each made in Your image to know agape love and fellowship with You.
Physical beings they, but with souls, spirits, and minds given freewill to serve and worship You.
They were not created identical but with dignity and equality before You.

They were given everything: life without fear or want, companionship, health, and joy.
An amazing home without tragedy, violence, quarrel, or storm.
They communed with You, Abba, without fear.
Satan whispered doubt to them of Your trustworthiness and they distanced themselves from You.
Not waiting to talk to You, in disobedience, they ate the one fruit they did not need. [3]

When You created them both male and female, the eternal covenant with them was made.
You would be their Caregiver and they would not want.
They would be Your children and would fellowship with You in the Garden Eden.
Sadly, their disobedience came at a high cost. [4]
Disobedience tore them away from this fellowship, Abba, for You <u>must</u> remain separated from sin.

The eternal covenant they did break, yet You did not.
The punishment for their sin did not immediately take their lives but made them mortal.
They could not live in Eden any longer where the Tree of Life still grows.
They lost their immortality, garden home, and their easy lives.
Yet, You remained their Caregiver and gave them less satisfying ways to worship [5]

Of Adam's sons, You favored Abel's gift over Cain's, so Cain killed his brother then argued with You.
His sin forever marked him, but you did not require his life. [6]
So, Abba, You gave Adam and Eve another son, Seth, to continue the covenant. [7]
Time did pass and Your patience and mercy turned to wrath.
All the world, the human race, You would destroy except a family of eight.

Did I say Your patience and mercy had ended?
Surely not for mankind had one-hundred years to repent while Noah built the ark.
The massive ark to house the genesis of their fresh start.
Yet, no one listened or believed Noah's plea for repentance.
So, You, Abba, ordered the animals into the ark that Noah and his family had stocked.

How heavy was Noah's heart when he and his family entered the ark last?
What sadness and trepidation did they feel when You sealed the massive door?
Rain fell for the first time, massive floodgates of water opened up and the people fled in fear.
The Flood that all cultures record filled the earth, covered the mountains and the giant ark floated.
You destroyed all of Your creation: plants and trees, animals and birds, men and women, <u>children</u> too.

Noah and his wife, their three sons and their wives lived in the ark for nearly a year.
Oh, but the day came when they and all the animals left the ark and moved into a silent world.
A world where fear existed between man and beast, animals were now food, and murder a capital offense.
Then You renewed Your covenant with them to be their God if only they'd be good.
Still their descendants had to choose between serving You or self, and sin was oft their choice.

Starting mankind anew, You gave them a covenant symbol like no other.
You set Your bow in the sky, a rainbow, for any to see after a rain.
A new covenant promise You made to never destroy the earth by flood again.
This covenant You have kept, Abba, no matter how man has come to vex.
Noah's sons: Japheth, Shem, and Ham, filled the earth, but You could not always delight in them. [8]

Descendants of three brothers, so family all, yet they distanced themselves from each other.
They made up our very human race, yet they could not live-in peace with one another.
Abba, I know this saddened You, but You continued the covenant through Shem's line. [9]
You called a man, Abram and his wife, Sari, to leave their family. And promised this aged childless
Couple a son and that Abram would be the father of children as numerous as the stars.

Abba, this covenant was sealed with a blood sacrifice of several animals and birds.
You visited Abram in a night vision and appeared as a smoking oven and flaming torch.
You passed between the pieces of their carcasses promising Abram's descendants much land.
You foretold Abram that he would be buried at a good old age, but his descendants would be strangers.
They would become enslaved in a foreign land for four hundred years before You would set them free.

Now when Abram was ninety-nine years old, You renewed Your promise to give them a son.
You changed his name to Abraham and Sarai to Sarah and marked it with a covenant in male flesh.
This blood covenant of male circumcision was to set them apart and distinguish them from others.
The promised son Isaac was not yet born but Abram had a son by Hagar, his wife's slave.
You name him Ishmael which means "God hears" for he was the slave son, not the promised son.

These two brothers could not live-in harmony, so Hagar was sent away with Ishmael.
But Abba You made promises to Hagar twice which You did keep and spared Ishmael's life.
He became the father of a mighty nation, twelve princes from his own flesh in one generation.
Yet, Isaac, the promised son and not the slave son, was Your covenant bearer.
You tested Abraham asking him to sacrifice Isaac and he obeyed, and You did spare Isaac too. [10]

Now Isaac had twin sons and the one called Jacob was a troubled man and the covenant bearer.
Your promise that Abraham would be the father of many nations proved true even before his death.
For Abraham not only had Ishmael and Isaac but six sons later in his life by another.
Keturah, Abraham's concubine, was not the mother of Abram's covenant son.
So, Abraham left all he had to Isaac, and sent these six east with gifts to start new lives apart. [11]

Genesis has many stories, but I strongly favor Joseph's.
Joseph was sold into slavery by his brothers including Judah the covenant bearer.
As a slave and jailed prisoner, Joseph trusted you through thirteen harsh years.
Then you allowed him to interpret Pharaoh's dream and Joseph advised Pharaoh to devise a plan.
Your plan positioned Joseph here at this time and he became the governor of Egypt.

As governor, he brought Jacob, and his extended family seventy strong to Egypt to escape a famine.
In time, Abraham's descendants became known as Israelites, as Jacob was renamed Israel.
Now Egypt's new Pharaoh feared the Israelites numbers and prosperity and made them slaves.
Even so, You blessed Your chosen people, and they multiplied to over two million strong.
As You said, for more than four-hundred years they were slaves in a land that was not their own. [12]

Eternal covenant keeper, how do You select, protect, and train ones for Your service?
There was, of course, Moses, one of the infant Israelite boys Pharaoh ordered slain.
His life was not only spared, but he was reared a well-educated prince in Egypt's royal palaces.
Yet, he murdered an Egyptian and fled to Midian, leaving his royal life.
From prince to lowly shepherd, You called him at eighty to go and set Your people free from slavery.

The story of the exodus is filled with ten plagues, loss, and the deaths of all of Egypt's first born.
But the Israelites were released from their slavery to go to their promised land. [13]
Sadly, they were a disobedient lot, and You would have destroyed them all and started new with Moses.
But, because of Moses' intercession, You did spare them but did not let their elders enter the good land.
They wandered forty years in the wilderness, You buried Moses there, and Joshua became their leader. [14]

Yes, all the frightened elders of the land were gone, save Caleb and Joshua the two faithful spies.
Caleb, a descendant of Judah, was faithful and took his mountain as a strong man of eighty. [15]
Perez, one of Judah's sons, was the lineage covenant bearer of his generation.
Later, when the Israelites, despite being warned of the dangers of a king they wanted, You gave them Saul.
Saul was not the covenant bearer, and You took his kingship away and gave it to another. [16]

David, from Judah, was a shepherd boy, a musician, a poet, and a warrior and Your anointed. [17]
You made him the promise to always have a son to sit upon his throne. [18]
Abba, You called him a man after Your own heart, yet he was not a sinless man.
Of necessity he was a man of war, but also a polygamist, an adulterer, and a murderer.
Yet, when David confessed his sins, You forgave and forgot his ugly deeds. [19]

Amongst David's sons was a rapist, an insurrectionist, a murderer who was also an insurrectionist.
From his sons, Solomon, born to Bathsheba, known for his wisdom, rose to his father's throne.
Yet, he too was a polygamist who worshiped the false idols of his thousand wives. [20]
At Solomon's death, his kingdom was divided and only a few of his descendants were ever faithful. [21]
But through his son, Rehoboam, we trace the lineage of Joseph who You chose for Jesus' earthly father.

Abba, like Sarah, we hear little of the maternal covenant bearer in the lineage of Jesus. [22]
David's son, Nathan, was in Mary's lineage, the chosen mother to bring our Savior into the world.
Jesus Christ, the Covenant Bearer and Keeper, Your only Son who came to save and unite us.
The promise now fulfilled that David would always have a descendant on his royal throne.
Only Jesus, the Eternal Son, proved Himself worthy to hold the throne of His father David forever. [23]

Yes, due to their lineage through David, Mary and Joseph bore blood lines of human royalty.
So, Jesus was born human with royal bloodlines and was yet Eternal God.
Jesus Christ came as a babe in a manager and was later crucified between two thieves.
King Jesus who came, served, healed, and taught us about salvation and His Kingdom without end.
Jesus came obediently from heaven to die as the propitiation for our sins.

We know Mary pondered the events of Jesus' life and kept them in her heart including Simeon's prediction.
"Her soul to be pierced with a sword so the son she delivered could deliver her and us." [24]
Jesus, Heaven's Perfect Lamb, was the only acceptable sacrifice for our redemption.
God's only Son who came to save us and give us eternal life through His death and resurrection.
Still not finished with us, He returned to Your throne room to be our Advocate. [25]

Abba, You kept all Your covenants from the start and through the forty-generations from Abraham to Jesus,
So, it is why I trust the two promises given to me and mine.
As Your daughter I hold this promise true. ***"I give them eternal life,***
And they shall never perish; no one will snatch them out of My hand." [26]
For this, Abba, I fall down to worship and stretch out my arms in eternal praise to You.

The second promise I cling to and hold quite dear,
"Behold, He is coming with the clouds, and every eye will see Him, even those who
pierced Him; and all the tribes of the earth will mourn over Him. So, it is to be. Amen." [27]
So, it will be Abba that I will live with the Trinity forever on the New Earth with all You gather in.
This isn't just something pretty I believe, Eternal Covenant Keeper, it is what I know to be true.

Yes, in Christ's birth, life, crucifixion, and resurrection a new covenant with us was fulfilled.
Abba, You've kept this promise too. ***"To put Your law within us, and to write it on our hearts.***
You then will be our God and we will be Your people forever.
We will know You and You will forgive our iniquity and remember our sin no more." [28]
Now please delight in this Christmas 2020 worship, Holy Father, Your world without end. Amen.

Abba, Your saving grace is my knowledge and why I worship You this Christmas. All through the centuries, since creation You have kept all Your promises given to us who never deserved them. Through each generation since Adam and Eve Your covenant to restore the human race was maintained and fulfilled in Jesus Christ. Yet, with all the events of 2020, many that surely disappoint You, I rest assured that You are the Eternal Covenant Keeper, and I and mine are in Your hands, just as are all those who You have already gathered home.

It is sad that we look at ourselves and see only skin deep, and forget that You made us in Your image, and love us all the same. Just as the people in Noah's day didn't hear the message to repent, so many do not hear now, but it is with gratitude I know You won't signal the angels to prepare for Christ's return until all those in the Lamb's Book of Life respond to the call and are sealed for eternal life by the Holy Spirit.

It will soon be Christmas 2020, yet my thoughts don't stay on Christ's birth, but on His death for He came into the world to prepare the way for us to find You; live in You; and be received home how or whenever our sojourn on earth ends. Jesus is our Light on our journeys here; He advocates for us at Your throne; and it was He who paid for our restoration to You; and it is Christ's blood that purchased our robes of righteousness so we can stand at Your throne and be received and welcomed home. We can trust no one more with our lives than Jesus who died for us! It is through the Holy Spirit that we are sealed and who is our GPS home. Abba, Jesus, and the Holy Spirit, Hallelujah, world without end. Amen.

December 4-23, 2020

Remember Me!

Abba, when Jesus ate His last supper with His disciples the night of His arrest,
He did more than share a last meal with them.
He tried one last time to prepare them for His crucifixion and the days and nights ahead.
Yet, in their love for Him and how they wanted things to remain, they couldn't begin to understand.
Peter even took Jesus aside once and rebuked Him. *"Never, Lord. This will not happen to You."*
Jesus answered Peter then, ***"Get behind me, Satan! You are a stumbling block to Me;***
you do not have in mind the concerns of God, but merely your human concerns." [1]

He shared with the twelve their last traditional Jewish Passover meal.
He said to them, ***"I have earnestly wanted to eat this Passover with you before I suffer;***
for I tell you, I will not eat it again until it finds fulfillment in the kingdom of God." [2]
Jesus washed their feet that night, a servant's task which spoke of His commitment to them, to us.
Later, while they were eating dinner, Jesus announced, ***"Truly I tell you, one of you will betray me."***
Then Judas, the one who would betray Him, said, *"Surely you don't mean me, Rabbi?"*
And Jesus answered him, ***"You have said so."*** [3]

Now Satan had entered Judas, so Judas left the celebration to lead his evil betrayal.
Jesus remained with the eleven and settled the controversy of who would be the greatest.
He prayed for them and us that night for the days ahead for them and the days to come for us.
He celebrated with them the first Passover night when the Israelites' firstborns were spared in Egypt.
Yes, the death angel passed over the Israelites' doors covered with the blood of a sacrificed lamb.
Jesus would be our sacrificial lamb in the hours to come and He would pray for it to pass over Him.
Yet, it could not be any other way; this bitter cup only He could drink for you and me.

He told Peter too that Satan had asked to sift him as wheat and that he would deny him three times.
This too was unfathomable for Peter, who felt confident that he would not deny, but die with Jesus.
Even so, Peter received this word of encouragement from our LORD. ***"But I have prayed for you, Simon,***
That your faith may not fail. And when you have turned back, strengthen your brothers." [4]
Yet, Peter would not die that night for Jesus would not lose any of the faithful eleven.
No, they would go and tell the gospel message as eyewitnesses and die for Jesus in their time.
Only Judas was destined to die this night, and this by his own hand for all he betrayed.

At the Lord's table, Jesus gave them a new covenant to keep.
While they were eating, Jesus took bread, and when He had given thanks, He broke it and gave it to His disciples,
Saying, ***"Take and eat; this is My body given for you; <u>do this in remembrance of Me."</u>***
Then He took a cup, and when He had given thanks, He gave it to them, saying, ***"Drink from it, all of you.***
This is My blood of the covenant, which is poured out for many for the forgiveness of sins.
I tell you; I will not drink this fruit of the vine from now on until that day
When I drink it again, in My Father's kingdom with you." [5]

They finished their supper with a Passover hymn, then Jesus led them out to the Mount of Olives.
That night in the Garden of Gethsemane, Jesus prayed that He could be spared the cup of crucifixion.
However, from the beginning of the world, His death for us was meant to be and could not be passed over.
Now I've heard it said that as Jesus' loving Father, You would never ask Jesus to die in our stead.
Yet, it is this very sacrificial love that nailed my Jesus to the cross of Calvary.
You, as our loving Holy Father, must remain separated from sin and only Jesus' death would satisfy the cost.
Yes, Abba, I understand that the thousands of animals sacrificed only gave temporary remission from sin.

As our Loving Father, You did not want us separated from You for all eternity.
There needed to be one last perfect sacrifice and Jesus was obedient to meet this need.
Abba, what father, what brother wouldn't give their life to save a sister or a brother?
The plan of salvation needed a Savior to once and for all pay for the remission of mankind's sin.
I heard it said that Jesus would have sacrificed His life if I was the only one in need.
Yet, His obedience and sacrifice paid for the debt sin of all mankind including me.
And this free gift available to all who seek it must be received to be applied.

Abba, You made us eternal beings and wanted us to share our eternal life with You in the heavenlies.
Jesus made this possible when He went to the cross to pay the required cost of our sins.
I heard asked, "Why would our loving God condemn anyone to eternity without Him?"
The answer is You, Abba, don't. It is a choice of every man and woman to choose their eternal destination.
Death cannot separate us from You, Abba, if we accept the gift of salvation purchased by Jesus.
No special words need be prayed to be saved, just a simple confession of sin to You needs made.
Then the unsaved become one of the elect who will spend eternity with You.

I want to pause here, Abba, and write the answer to the question that came to my mind.
What does it mean "until it finds fulfillment in the kingdom of God"?
Revelation tells us that *"Christ's blood ransoms people from every tribe, tongue, and nation."* [6]
Jesus' blood, death, burial, and resurrection paid the sin debt He didn't owe,
And made salvation and restoration a free gift to any who will seek it.
But until all the saved are gathered home into the eternal kingdom, fulfillment of Jesus' work is not complete.
The fulfillment of Jesus' work will be celebrated when Jesus eats with all of His redeemed in heaven.

So, it is Abba that I remember Jesus and what He did for me upon the old, rugged cross.
I remember His cruel handling, torture, abuse, flogging, humiliation, pain and suffering.
Oh, yes, sweet Jesus, Your agony is not lost on me for I remember Resurrection Sunday.
The tomb could not hold You and You conquered sin and death for me.
You laid down Your life but took it up again and now advocate for me at Abba's throne. [7]
This is my remembrance praise for this Resurrection Sunday.
Herein Abba, Jesus, and the Holy Spirit be glorified. Amen.

"Take and eat; this is My body given for you.
Remember Me each time you do this.
Drink from it, all of you.
This is the new covenant in My blood,
Which is poured out for many for the forgiveness of sins. [8]*

Rhoda Fegan April 3, 2021

"Greater love has no one than this, that one lay down his life for his friends." John 15:13

I sing in the shadow of Your wings because You are my help.
My soul clings to You; Your right hand upholds me. Psalm 63:7-8

The LORD will guide you always;
He will satisfy your needs in a sun-scorched land and will strengthen your frame.
You will be like a well-watered garden, like a spring whose waters never fail. Isaiah 58:11

"Innocent"

"I was falsely arrested, tried, beaten, mocked, and flogged.
Unlike my accusers and captors, I had kept the laws and was sinless.
Claiming My identity in Truth was to My accusers a crime worthy of death.
They thrust a crown of thorns into My scalp in mockery of My identity.
For them, My innocence and crime were intertwined."

"Judas, one of My own disciples, had conspired with the priests to betray Me.
He sold Me out for the sum paid for a slave and led them to where I often prayed.
My other followers and friends deserted Me that dark night for fear of their own arrest.
Days earlier, they bravely vowed to follow Me to death, now, they ran and hid in fear.
In My human form, innocent, I bore the weight of the sin of all mankind."

"My eyes were so swollen from My beatings that I could barely see.
Relentless pain forced tears from My eyes but couldn't clear the blood pooled in them.
I suffered from sleep deprivation, blood loss, dehydration, and shock.
Beaten, bruised, and swollen with open wounds, I was unrecognizable as a human.
Yet, willingly, I carried a criminal's crossbeam and was mocked until I fell beneath its weight."

"My clotted wounds were ripped open when My blood soaked garments were pulled off.
Pain screamed from every nerve fiber in My naked human body.
My wrists were pierced through with crude rusted spikes to your crossbeam.
My feet were forced together, and a single spike was driven through them into your cross.
My raw and bleeding back felt the splinters of the rough wood of a very old and brutal cross."

"For six hours I rode the saddle of your cross forcing My body up to take in a deep breath.
I had to pull against the spikes in My wrists and push against the spike that pierced My feet.
This was how I satisfied My lungs and heart's demand for oxygen.
This is how I was able to speak and keep My spirit in its human body all those agonizing hours.
I knew pain like no other, for I was innocent suffering for your sin and not My own."

"I came to mankind as an innocent babe to Mary and Joseph.
I learned Joseph's trade and had the calloused hands of a carpenter.
I used those hands in My earthly ministry with compassion.
I fed the multitudes; healed the sick; and restored sight to the blind.
The lame lost their disabilities; missing limbs were made whole; and the paralyzed walked."

"Before Caiaphas and the Sanhedrin no two accusers could falsify charges sufficient to condemn me.
Only when I said the truth of being the son of God was I sentenced to death under Jewish law.
Tried before Pontius Pilate, the Roman prefect, I was found innocent.
Sent to be tried by Herod, I remained silent and did not demonstrate My power before him.
A second time before Pilate, My freedom was in the offering."

"Oh, but this could not be for I was born to suffer and die upon your cross.
So, the priests in the crowd amongst those I had shown mercy stirred a chant.
'Release Barabbas' they chanted, and *'Crucify Jesus'* and the crowd easily took up their refrain.
The week before, the crowd shouted "Hosanna" and laid palm branches and their coats along My path.
I had triumphantly entered Jerusalem on an untrained colt knowing My fate even as I heard their praise."

"Yet, *'Crucify Him'* saw Me on a labored and forced march with your cross upon My back.
Out the gates of Jerusalem and up Golgotha hill to the place of the crucified.
The priests had the scriptures and knew the prophecies regarding My first coming.
Trained to expect Me, they didn't apply any of all they knew to Me.
They zealously wanted to protect their livelihoods and wealthy positions from change."

"They weren't watching for their king in the humble circumstances as the prophets foretold.
They, like My disciple Judas, wanted a conquering King upon a noble steed.
They wanted armies of angels to destroy Rome and leave them to their status.
Yet, I did not come to conquer what My Father had created and owned.
I came to restore His children to spiritual fellowship with Us in the world."

"The plea, 'Father, stop this!' never came to My mind or lips.
From the beginning of time, this moment had been planned.
My suffering and crucifixion, the required sacrifice for mankind was now fulfilled.
Yes, upon your cross I finished Our plan for salvation and restoration for sinful man.
Yet, in all the hardest part I bore wasn't pain or impending death, but separation from the Father."

"Before the universe was created; mankind placed in it; and time started, We had been One.
I was in the Father; He was in Me; and His Holy Spirit was in Us.
Leaving heaven for earth, this distant relationship of Us was not the same.
Yet, I could bear it through prayer, for in prayer I still felt the connection of Us.
But upon your cross the Father's holiness could not allow any connection between Us."

"In those hours, I was not the Son, but Sin, and Father and His Holy Spirit couldn't look at Me.
A dark curtain fell around the place of the skull blotting out the sun midday.
My Father couldn't look upon what I had become to rescue and restore you.
How do I explain the pain of having the unity of eternal love in Us ripped away to you?
Yet, it is why I allowed Myself to be nailed to your cross in your stead."

"That which We had, and I would return to was what I willingly gave up to die for you.
If I had not paid your sin debt with My life, you could never come to Us.
You could never share in eternal unity in the divine but would have had to remain separated from Us.
Now beloved child, you can choose to have My payment of your sin applied to your sin debt.
Then your debt which you cannot pay will be paid in full, "Tetelestai" and your account closed."

"My death was painful physically, mentally, and My Soul and Spirit were tortured by separation.
So, beloved, don't choose separation from Us, but choose life in Us here and for eternity.
Yes, here you will face difficulties, illness, loss of loved ones and even your own death.
But, whatever your circumstances, rejoice for I have overcome death.
And beloved, you will never face difficult times on your own for Our Holy Spirit is ever with you."

"In Us, when your earthly life ends, your new life in an eternal glorified body begins.
You will be reunited forever with loved ones who live in Us.
You will delight in the unity of Us for all eternity.
Because I died for you, I advocate for you at My Father's throne daily.
Seek Us now and you will find Us and live forever as We originally planned."

"When I said from your cross, 'Tetelestai' (*'It is finished.'*) I was not finished because I took up My life again.
But the plan of salvation and restoration was finished.
Choose to be saved and restored to Us and finish your earthly course here in Us.
Eternity is not far off and someday soon time will be complete.
Let not My suffering be in vain but gain eternal life through Me."

"You, beloved, were created as an eternal being.
Your fragile earthly body cannot last for all eternity.
But your essence, mind, soul, and spirit will transfer to a body glorified.
Your eternal body can live painfully separated from Us in hell or joyfully with Us in Paradise.
Let only Satan and his demons remain separated from Us. Choose unity in Us, beloved."

June 7, 2021

My Jesus, You truly were innocent for the guilt of the sin You bore for me was indeed all mine. It was a debt I was never capable of clearing from my account. It was a debt I could not pay or work off to satisfy. I debt I was not even worthy to be forgiven for on my own. But by Your sacrifice it is a debt that was paid in full when I accepted Your death on my behalf, when I was covered by Your redeeming blood. You were innocent and I was not! Yet in You I am now forgiven and my debt forgotten. Forever and always Precious Savior, Thank you for the life I now have and for the eternal life in a glorified body in the Trinity which I now claim through You. Amen.

Chapter Three

Praise and Worship

How can these pieces not be some of my favorites?
These pieces are praise and worship at their highest form – worthship.

Adoration

How awesome, O LORD, is Thy throne and footstool.
The breath of Your court is counted in miles,
and its spectacular beauty can only be captured in glimpses.
The panorama is alive and ever changing
and touched by sunrises and sunsets that no man may see.
It is a place of comfort and rest for angels to revive their spirits
as they come and go from the earth to care for man.

What is man that he can behold Thy throne room and contemplate it grandeur,
then walk away untouched by the understanding that You alone are God?
In these mountains and canyons, in the range of environs of all Your earth
I feel You LORD and am at peace to know that you care for me
Above all You have created.
Your presence comforts me and soothes away the voices of darkness and fear.
Although I may walk without company, I am never alone.

My body may falter but my spirit soars within me
As I instantly recall the site of Your Grand Canyon.
I hear Your voice and see the great slabs of rock form and rise,
And watch as Your finger passes through the valley,
Then see the water rush to fill in the gap left behind.

Who is man that you have recorded proof for him in rock,
Water, plants, trees, flowers, and all the animals of the world
Your formidable power and still he does not bow down
To acknowledge and worship You as God?

I have given birth and watched as their new lives emerged from my womb
And called it a miracle for no thought or action was required
For me to shape the babies I conceived and cradled within me.
How I have loved the gifts You gave me from my own womb,
But never once instructed their hearts to beat,
Their lungs fill, their bodies grow, or their minds learn.
Yet, covered by Your own love for them and watched over my angels,
My prayers were answered, and they became fine adults who confessed Your Name.

This Passover season I am moved to heights of awe that I have no words
To voice the praise that would equal what I feel.
I was born, gave birth, and now cut Shirley's cord on our shared birthday.
I saw Your mighty Grand Canyon and learned its breath and dimensions.
My spirit recognizes You as its Sovereign LORD and Master,
And I will bow down to worship Your majesty.

Father, does this piece speak well to the wonder of seeing the Grand Canyon, and cutting Shirley's umbilical cord? I remember that day so well. I took the day off from work to celebrate my day, and to celebrate the day more for it was my daughter, Tammy's, birthday too. It was cold, pouring rain, workers were replacing gutters on my house, and the phone rang, and I was invited to my great-niece's imminent birth. April 21, 2000, I remember well. I wrote on this piece, <u>please LORD watch over this child that has taken root in my heart as my very own, although she is my great niece and not my child.</u>

2017: Abba, I can offer You praise for she is alive and well and seventeen, and I still have hope that she will rise above her birth circumstance because You are answering that day's prayer. I still remember, LORD, the awe, the wonder, and the fullness of my heart these words tried to offer in adoration to You for all You are and provide. Glory and honor still pours from my heart for a cold and miserable day that was so much more than the weather. Love forever and ever, life everlasting in Jesus' holy name, Amen.

2022: Shirley is married and working as a Donato's store manager. Trusting You LORD with her life still. Amen

Absolutely

God's knowledge is absolute.
God's power is absolute.
God's love is absolute.
God absolutely wants to hear from you
About everything in your life.

"Be anxious for nothing,
*But in **everything** by prayer and supplication*
*With **thanksgiving** let your requests*
Be made known to God. And, the peace of God,
Which surpasses all comprehension, shall
Guard your hearts and minds in Christ Jesus." [1]

God knows what you need.
He wants you to acknowledge what you need
To Him about everything with praise.
Then, His peace can replace your anxiety.
A nice trade indeed.

So, then keep nothing back from God.
How can you anyway when He already knows your heart?
Believe there are no can'ts with God
For with God there are no limits to the possibilities.
Say, with Paul, *"I can do all things through*
Him who strengthens me." [2]

Then, remember that the will of God will never lead you
Where the grace of God cannot keep you.
God is with you through all the uncertainties of life,
Abiding with you to grow you, absolutely.

From God to you through me – keeping you in my prayers with love.
March 23, 2003

Dear Jesus

I am so in love with You, LORD and now declare it.
O LORD Jesus, before the world was created,
You shared glory with God, Our Father.
Angels bowed down to you in glad adoration.
You were God's only Son, His delight before creation.

Sin entered the world through Adam and Eve.
Yet, in the fullness of time you came to earth as a baby.
Angels declared Your birth to a world trapped in darkness.
And You became our eternal light.
God affirmed His love for us on that night.

You are now my light, my love, my life.
My soul could be trapped in strife,
Grief, concerns, any of life's sorrows.
Yet not, as these are life burdens that You carry for me each day,
As I seek the joy and comfort of being your child and offer praise.

God tested Abraham's faith when he called for Isaac to be sacrificed.
In obedience he journeyed forward to pay the price,
And placed his son upon an altar.
But, before the blade made its way into his tender flesh,
You substituted a perfect lamb and gave this father and son rest.

When the children of Israel, left their Egyptian captivity,
All the firstborn of the land were to be sacrificed.
But the death angel passed over all the houses covered
In the blood of a perfect lamb and so God spared
Their animals, sons, and daughters.

When Cain killed his brother Abel,
his blood cried out for recognition and retribution.
You gave up your life on Calvary and Your blood
paid for my redemption and forgiveness.
No other lamb was worthy to be the final sacrifice.

You crushed death and rose again.
and sit beside the Father as my Savior and Friend.
Yet a little while and I will kneel at Your nail scarred feet,
and feel Your forgiving touch as Your nail scarred hands bid me rise.
Dressed in robes of white bought by Your blood, I will see Your glory with eternal eyes.

2006

Heart's Desire

My heart's desire is to see and hear you Father
In the trees clothed in leaf, flower, fruit, and seed.
You are in the rustling of summer leaves, the barren trees of winter,
And you never leave the evergreen.

My heart's desire is to see and hear you Father
For You are in the valleys fresh with dew and life.
You are in the mountains that stand guard over all the earth,
And in the deep chill of winter's long barren nights.

My heart's desire is to see and hear you Father
In rushing waters and ocean waves as they break.
You are in cascading waterfalls, swamps, and puddles,
In icicles, frozen ponds, and crystalline blue lakes.

My heart's desire is to see and hear you Father
With nesting birds as You keep them through cold and stormy nights.
You soar with the eagles and mark the flights
Of each hummingbird, sparrow, vulture, hawk, and kite.

My heart's desire is to see and hear you Father
In the mewing of a calf or kitten, and puppies as they play.
You are with the beasts of the fields as they search for fodder
And with the lion as it stalks its prey.

My heart's desire is to see and hear you Father
In the undulations of fish in the various waters where they roam.
You swim with dolphins, porpoises, and whales,
And guide sharks, piranha, and alligators to their homes.

My heart's desire is to see and hear you Father
In the sun as it kisses the earth with light.
You strung the planets and the stars, and you see the moon
By its measure and not just in the stillness of the night.

My heart's desire is to see and hear you Father
In the birth of all things, great and small.
You inhabit my praise and know my name,
And always answer when I call.

My heart's desire is to see and hear you Father for
You are the thread woven into the fabric of my life.
You will be with me in the final goodbye of mortal days
And then will open my eyes to wondrous new sights.

It is then my heart's desire will be fulfilled for
I will see You, Father and pray I hear You say,
"Well done, good and faithful daughter.
You have come home to stay."

2006

Abba, thank you for this hope that comes from Your love. I am Yours now and forever. My brain can't quite comprehend it but my heart is all for it. Keep me living and growing in Your peace. Amen.

Blessings

I can't count my blessings.
They are like grains of sand,
Too numerous and often overlooked.

But what my eyes see, my ears hear,
What my brain perceives
Always brings praise to my lips.

You have taught my heart to look for them.
You are worthy of my praise.
LORD, you are worthy of all praise.

You gave me forgiveness and forgetfulness
After the cross and prayed for me before.
You lead by the way of love.

You are still a God of miracles.
I have had them in my life.
When I need them now, I am not afraid to ask.

I know that You are always ready to hear from me.
I can trust You with my burdens and cares.
Your mercy and love for me is new every day.

Your word is my light,
Solace for the past, peace for today,
And hope for tomorrow.

April 6, 2008

God Knows

God knows us because He made us.
He knows us better than we know ourselves.
If we allow Him, His presence is always with us.
He goes with us on our journeys through life.

We look and see an obstacle – a can't.
God sees a way, a path – a can.
We don't see our potential – what we can accomplish.
God knows what we can do with His Holy Spirit living inside of us.

He doesn't ask us to win the race.
He doesn't ask us to run.
He doesn't ask us to walk.
He asks us to fall in step beside Him.

Each day has its own joy.
We must find that joy and praise Him.
We must trust Him when we don't see His plan.
We must finish the race at His side.

The power that created the universe.
The power that parted the Red Sea is the power that saved us.
It is the same power we have each day.
We have no need to journey alone.

November 30, 2015

Abba, I am reminded of the conversation in the rear seat of my little Ronda some years ago between newly saved six year old Lauryn and her three year old sister Abbi. You will remember that Lauryn was sweetly advising Abbi to give her heart to Jesus and let Jesus come and live in her heart. Abbi said, "No, thank you. It will hurt."

She too was later saved and baptized and learned that it didn't hurt at all. Learned that it really felt just right to have that God-shaped void in her heart filled with Your Holy Spirit.

Now all of the original six grandchildren are saved, four baptized, and my newest, little five year old Nora, is learning about Jesus in Awana on Wednesday night at church and on children's church television on Sunday mornings at home. Thank you, Abba, that they are yours and that Nora too will be Yours too for all eternity.

Child of God

I am Your child, oh God.
Your blood cleansed me and now flows through my veins.
Your love and joy courses through my nerves,
wakening me to feel Your presence.

Your words and thoughts fill my mind casting out doubt,
Opening me to hope and joy,
And praise naturally flows from my lips.

My heart is filled with Your love and compassion,
Renewing me at the coming of each day,
And I willingly serve as You direct.

My hands and feet are lovingly compelled to go and serve where You lead.
My eyes see and ears hear the wonder of Your impressive creation,
And causes my spirit to soar to the heavens, so I can kneel before Your throne.

The enemy may stalk me, send fiery darts of fear and lies,
But Christ is my Shield and Defender and fear and lies
Are subject to His love and truth.

I dwell within an earthly frame that must age and weaken,
Yet I grow stronger in mind and spirit. Illness may stalk me,
And death may lay claim, but since You call me Your beloved, I will not be afraid.

When my journey leads through valleys dark,
I will lift my eyes up and call on my Savior, Jesus Christ,
My advocate at Your very throne.

I will rest there in His arms of love until restored,
Or snuggle there a moment longer in my resurrected body.
Then all of the unimagined joys of heaven will be mine.

I live in You, Abba, saved through Jesus' sacrifice, adopted into the
Eternal Kingdom and filled by the Holy Spirit.
I am complete now in the Trinity and heir to heaven's riches and joy.
Now and forever Your beloved daughter.

I am a child of God.
Sunday Sermon September 17, 2017

In You

I have You every hour for You are always near.
You are less than a prayer away.
You meet all my needs, giving me many wants.
I often have before I ask.

I call upon You sometimes without words.
And You hear and answer me by name.
You are the Great I am, I live because You live.
I live each day in the power and blessing of Your love.

I am made perfect in my weaknesses by You.
By Your strength I face each day.
I look to Your, my LORD, my Rock and my Shield.
You are my destination, my eternal home.

You gave Your life for me and became my life.
I am complete only in Your beauty.
I cannot be lost for You saved me
I am ever held secure in Your loving Hands.

O LORD, my Creator, I feel Your unconditional love.
I trust in You alone, my Redeemer and my Groom
No matter my state, I am whole in You.
In You alone I have hope, with each breath I am satisfied.

June 28, 2015, bulletin
November 30, 2015

Jesus our Veteran

Praise to Jesus who was and is divine before, during, and after time.
Come to know Jesus Christ who is the Son of God and Son of Man forever.
Praise Jesus our Savior, our advocate at God's right hand and our eternal King.
Open your heart to Jesus who bridges the gap between deity and humanity.
Praise Jesus whose eternal glory was shrouded when He came to earth to become our light.
Reach out to our Savior whose Three in One divine glory we saw at His baptism.

Praise Jesus whose Shekinah glory was witnessed on the mountaintop by Peter, James and John.
Know the Father through the Son who spoke both times,
"This is My Son, whom I love and am well pleased. Listen to Him!" [1]
The gap between deity and humanity momentarily suspended with Moses and Elijah there.
Feel the glory and revel in the worship shared between Jesus and His disciples on the holy mountain.
See Jesus' radiance revealed not reflected by His human form—a foretaste of His eternal glory divine.
Understand the death penalty for seeing Shekinah glory was removed because Jesus bridged the gap.

Remember Jesus laid down His shared glory in the Eternal and took up our cross.
He came as a sweet babe and grew into a sinless man and stood in the gap for us.
Jesus, lowly, beaten and bloodied Jesus, crucified upon Golgotha's hill to pay a debt He did not owe.
His human body in a borrowed tomb laid to be raised on the third day as He foretold.
Yes, Jesus came to earth from the Eternal the perfect sacrifice to end the need for sacrifices.
He left the throne room of heaven and became the ultimate priest to direct us to the Father.

Jesus abolished the need for earthly temples as our hearts are now the temple of His Holy Spirit.
He came in unconditional love to forever share with us the love known only in the Trinity.
Beloved surrender to Jesus our Veteran and Coming King who won the war against the enemy.
In Him receive eternal life to meet your lifelong need of the Creator.
Then, with all the others, stand at the door of heaven and wait for its opening and your welcome home.
Worship and give honor, love, and glory to God through Jesus our Redeemer now and for eternity.

To Obedient Jesus who volunteered to come and serve on our behalf and in our stead, give praise.
To Sinless Jesus who won the battle of the Wilderness against Satan showing us the way, give honor.
To Healer Jesus who overcame disease, disabilities, and death in His ministry, give love.
To Teacher Jesus who didn't leave us alone but left us His disciples and the Holy Spirit, give glory.
Remember Jesus who won the lone battle of the Garden of Gethsemane against His humanity.
Praise Jesus who could have called for angelic reinforcements but stayed the course.

Thank you, Jesus, for enlisting and leading in the earthly battle for the souls of the beloved.
Thank you for gaining victory over our enemies, Satan, sin, and death.
Lead on Jesus and thank you for Your sacrifice.
We give our all to You, Jesus, LORD of angel armies, our Supreme Commander.
Jesus, You ascended into heaven to be our advocate and to prepare an eternal home for us.
We will wait and serve faithfully for time to be complete when we can lay our rewards at Your feet.

November 21, 2016

Elohim

Holy, holy, holy the great One in Three.
High King of Heaven who created the universe and me.
Jesus Lover of all creation poured out for me.
Holy Spirit given and living through me.

Father God You called creation into being
And executed the plan for its restoration.
Jesus how difficult the task to leave glory behind
To come and die to save mankind?

God's plan called for one perfect sacrifice.
Jesus was the only one yet came willingly to pay the price.
The Holy Spirit too was asked to do more.
Asked to come and dwell in all who find peace in Elohim.

Like ancient clay vessels You saw past my marred surface.
You restored my brokenness with Your touch and made me whole again.
You took this earthen tabernacle cleansed and filled it with Your presence.
You made me worthy to serve Your lost creation to encourage their journey to restoration.

Your faithfulness then is my confidence.
For when my soul was lost in darkness You came to be its light.
You are always with me now, but life is not without its trials.
Even so, You come and speak peace and I am not afraid.

Now my heart clings to the but nots [1] and speaks to praise You.
Not just to You Elohim, but to those who need to hear of You.
The Eternal Day can't come until all to be saved and are gathered safely in.
Then time and creation will be complete, and we can kneel at Elohim's feet.

Great High King of Heaven, Jesus Lover of my soul, the Living Spirit filling me,
I am laying down my troubles. Friends, family, all I bring to Your thrones. [2]
Now I lay me down at Your feet to worship for the night won't last.
Then You raise me up, and I will go out with the joy of the LORD and wait for the Eternal day.

Amen
September 16, 2018

[1] *We are hard pressed on every side, but not crushed; perplexed, but not in despair;
persecuted, but not abandoned; struck down, but not destroyed. 2 Corinthians 4:8*

The Trinity's Amazing Love

Amazing Love was shared between the Trinity in the Before.
The Three in One wanted to share Their love and prepared a plan.
God spoke one word and the universe formed.
God was not done, oh no, because the universe still expands.

Amazing Love a solar system strewn.
In its expanse a favored planet flourished just right for all mankind.
God, then, created Adam, the first man of flesh and bone created He,
And God breathed in his nostrils and Adam became a living being.

Amazing Love created Adam from the dust of the ground,
making him in the image of the Trinity in Their own likeness he.
Now God planted a garden in the east that was pleasing to the eye,
And all yielded fruit save one for the sinless man to eat.

Amazing Love placed Adam in the garden called Eden with two special trees,
The Tree of Life from which Adam could eat.
The second tree, the Tree of the Knowledge of Good and Evil,
was not given to the man for food, its pleasing fruit not for him to eat.

Amazing Love saw the need for His creation to share his life with a like kind being.
So, God placed Father Adam into a slumber deep.
While he slept God took his rib and made him a perfect helpmate.
Mother Eve He created a suitable helpmate to share Adam's needs.

Amazing Love closed the flesh of Adam with his rib restored.
He was introduced to Eve, and he called her woman, for she was taken out of him.
How idyllic was their life in Eden then, carefree children nurtured in their garden home.
They enjoyed fellowship in the cool of the day with their Creators.

Amazing Love created them and gave them everything to live in eternal bliss and innocence.
Sadly, Satan came to spoil their garden home, and sin came to them and us.
You know the story from the Tree of Knowledge of Good and Evil they each did disobediently eat.
Our once sinless parents now knew they were naked and did hide themselves with leaves.

Amazing Love came to Eden that fateful day and God did spare the pair.
He sacrificed animals to clothe them and to teach them that blood sacrifice is the price of sin.
However, now unclean, they could not stay, so God cast them from His garden beautiful.
They could not stay and eat from the Tree of Life and live in sin eternally condemned.

No, Amazing Love was not surprised by their disobedience, and They did not abandon them.
In time God sent Jesus, Part of the Three in One, to be the perfect final sacrifice for them and me.
Jesus because of His love quite willingly paid the extraordinary price to restore the pair to fellowship.
Through Jesus' sacrifice we all too may choose the gift of eternal life and be restored to Them.

Amazing Love remains the same and eternity beckons all.
All may elect salvation because Christ's blood covered the cost of everyone's sins and fall.
Once saved all the beloved will someday eat from the Tree of Life as God always planned.
Amazing Love still saves! Eternity Awaits! Come join the fellowship today!

January 28, 2018

Abba, thank you for the gifts of Your amazing love. Therefore, we do not lose heart. Though outwardly we are wasting away, yet inwardly we are being renewed day by day. For our light and momentary troubles are achieving for us an eternal glory that far outweighs them all. <u>So, we fix our eyes not on what is seen, but on what is unseen. For what is seen is temporary, but what is unseen is eternal. 2 Corinthians 4:16-18.</u> Praise, Father, Son, and Holy Spirit. Your world without end. Amen!

You will keep us in perfect peace, whose mind stays on You, because we trust in You.
Isaiah 26.3

Creation: Accident or Intent?

Have you ever noticed the variety of life God created?
It is not limited or boring, no not at all indeed.
Some creatures swim while others fly or just move about on a variety of legs.
And life on this unique little planet includes all kinds of trees and other vegetation.
No God of Creation you declare but wait a moment and let me proceed.
For creation to be an accident, my friend, takes greater faith for me you see.
Accidents seem to me to leave a mess, so thank you Father for two eyes instead of three.
My praise for walking upright in this complicated body I call me.

The beauty of a rose by accident would surely be enough.
But I confess to love the beauty of orchids, tulips, daisies, mums, and the clematis too.
Then there are trees as in mighty oaks, maples, and sycamores, and the giant redwoods too!
Balsams, firs, and pine trees and if only one kind of tree shouldn't it be the Christmas tree?
Oh, but then, my friend, you think Christ's birth that brought us Christmas is just a myth.
Now all these types of trees are surely good, but wouldn't we miss all the ones that bear our fruit?
And all the ornamental trees too are nice. But trees do so much more.
Trees absorb pollutants and odors, shade and cool our streets, and give us the oxygen of life.

Now I've gone on about these living things but let me add the amazing cacti of the globe.
How amazing vegetation is that it survives and thrives in all the environs of your accidental world.
Forgive me, my friend, for going on and on, but there is so much to appreciate.
Buds and blooms on trees and shrubs in color, not just in black and white!
How amazing too that in winter many seem dead but in spring burst forth in flower, leaf, and fruit.
But then this is not the standard for we have trees called evergreens.
I'm done with trees, but what of crops? Surely you wouldn't miss rice, barley, oats, wheat, or rye?
What think you of sweet-buttered corn? What's a movie without popcorn?

You want me to stop talking about vegetative life, but my list really can go further.
Ok, my friend, I'm done with vegetation but what about life that comes with fur or feathers?
Robins, cardinals, sparrows, blue jays, wrens, and hummingbirds brighten my yard.
But I think I would miss parakeets, parrots, cockatiels, and the like.
And where would we be without the vultures and their kind?
Without the bald eagle what would our nation's symbol be?
The world would be hungrier if there were no chickens, turkeys, ducks, or geese!
Oh, the beauty of the majestic swan, and even the blue heron that once feasted from my pond!

Some folks don't like reptiles, alligators, or crocodiles, including snakes, but they all have their place.
Insects seem to be all over the place, but I appreciate dragonflies and butterflies.
Mosquitos aren't my thing, but bats and frogs and other creatures appreciate such things.
Would childhood be the same without ladybugs, or the flickering lightning bug?

And what about the honeybee and what it gives to us?
Termites, locusts, flies, fleas, ticks, and lice might make me wonder why the need?
Do not let me forget to mention katydids, grasshoppers, tiny ants, and the amazing praying mantis!
Forgive my list it could grow longer, but I do not believe they came about by cosmic accident.

Now let me think of what lives in flowing waters, lakes, oceans, and streams.
Fish and all that fill the waters great and small are amazing, my friend, and not food for me!
Yes, I fear any shark, but whales, porpoise and dolphins are pleasing for me to see.
Then there are manatees, jellyfish, sting rays, starfish, seahorses and so much more that are amazing.
Lobsters, shrimp, oysters, and the like don't appeal to me, but to pearls I do defer.
Do not let me forget sea turtles, eels, squid, and the eight-armed octopus.
And, let me remark how amazing that some need fresh water and others salt to live.
I appreciate all who dive to see these creatures, but I like seeing them in sparkling glass aquariums.

Should I mention cows and pigs or goats and sheep? Surely our diets do not really rely on them?
I don't like to think of them as living creatures when I eat a burger, roast, or chop.
So, let me turn our attention to mules and donkeys, and the beauty created in the horse.
Some are working animals for sure, but horses seem a special creature with many men.
Then there are the creatures that give us love and companionship.
Thank you, LORD, for every dog and cat that has been mine.
The world would be a sadder place without puppy dogs and kittens.
Squirrels, raccoons, beavers, hamsters, gerbils, bunnies, and the like were surely not an accident.

There are the large animals too – elephants, giraffes, gorillas, baboons, and hippopotamuses.
Oh, but wait what of black bears, brown bears, polar bears, lions, tigers, and panda bears?
What of kangaroos with their baby Joey pouches? How many types of monkeys exist?
I like seeing these animals at zoos and will travel to explore botanical gardens too.
Then let's see there is this creature called man that is about.
We are such trouble, LORD, and in this life we struggle.
We are not like the animals I've listed for we were created with an eternal soul.
True like them, our bodies must perish, but then our eternal soul is released.

So, my friend, believe what you will believe. Accept the story that the universe exploded
On the scene without intelligent design. The world was once deemed flat too.
I am no mathematician or scientist but the odds of this seem most unreasonable.
The eternal soul in you I know yearns to find the answer.
Your eternal soul seeks my Divine Creator, LORD, and Master.
I'll pray for you to believe that you didn't come about by accident but were intended.
An eternal body waits for my eternal soul to join it in the happy ever after.
Careful now my friend, the immortal soul of non-believers lives forever too – in a lake of fire.

April 26, 2019

Abba, I truly love this piece. It is a bit on the glib side but speaks the truth for I don't understand how anyone cannot believe that You created our world with intent and purpose. Bind Satan, Holy Spirit, from letting the concept that the world was created as a cosmic accident continue to be accepted and believed. Thank you, Abba, for creating such an amazing world for my home now and in its new form for all eternity. Your world without end, Abba, now and forever. Praise and Amen.

The Wonder of You

You were omnipotent before You created the universe!
With one word, universe, You spoke the universe into creation.
Mankind doesn't appreciate the complexity of our galaxy.
It is more complicated then, we, Your human creation can understand.
Your preexistence and omnipotence is the wonder of You.

More complicated still is Your Three in One presence.
You are the Triune Godhead – Father, Son, and Holy Spirit.
We were created in Your image – body, mind, and soul.
Eternal beings, we, shaped by Your hand and filled with Your breath.
Our existence speaks to Your power, the wonder of You.

The love of the Trinity created all that exists including our first parents.
Your love was such that they spoke to Your face to face.
Satan's lies had them betray Your love and they so they couldn't live in Eden.
Yet, they were not homeless nor completely on their own.
Your mercy and grace is the wonder of You.

You set apart Abraham and his descendants for Yourselves.
You gave them human leaders, statues, and rules to obey.
You, the eternal God, wanted them to worship You alone.
Your conquered nations before them, protected, and cared for them.
This great tenderness to such a vast people is the wonder of You.

Their obedience and love was all You asked of Your beloved people.
They were to behave as Your elect, not like the fallen Canaanites.
Yet they succumbed to pagan service and crafted images to worship.
They worshiped and prayed to idols they handmade from sticks and stones.
You gave them prophets to guide them who they ignored, and this too is the wonder of You.

Generation after generation You strived with Your beloved children.
They would not follow Your will for them but lived to please themselves.
In time, Jesus came as a babe to live with them yet in divine perfection.
Jesus in human flesh bought the commandments to life to free us.
Jesus' coming, His teachings, and healings was also the wonder of You.

Jesus chose followers to learn and to teach the way to heaven through Him.
Then in the ripeness of time allowed Himself to die for the sin of all mankind.
Jesus paid our death penalty and rose again over death victorious.
Death could not keep Him, so He became our means of escape too.
This Abba is the wonder of Jesus and the wonder of You.

Now Abba each of us can choose to repent from our sins and live in Him.
Living here in Christ is no sacrifice for we have the Holy Spirit.
The third member of the Trinity who comes to live in us when we choose Christ.
Life here then isn't necessarily all ease, but the journey ends in Heaven.
Our restoration and eternal destination is the wonder of You.

This earth in all its sorrow is not our true home.
Mortal bodies that decline with age and illness are not all we have.
Buried in a grave and forgotten within a few generations is not the end.
We in Christ Jesus soar in bodies glorified and come to You.
Eternal life in Paradise is also the wonder of You.

My Holy Father, Jesus Savior, and the Holy Spirit hear these words of praise.
We are Your creation restored and bow down to worship You.
I hear eternal anthems, Abba, music unlike heard on our fallen planet.
Thank you for calling me and mine, restoring us, and preparing a place for us.
This too, Three in One, is the wonder of You.

The Coronavirus 19 saga is Yours, Abba, please rebuke it, draw a line and let it infect no further. You stopped plaques before, Abba, protect Your children once again. We who love You know we can't survive this well without You. Abba, save us. Fear cannot have us, and Satan cannot steal our joy. We, Abba, are Your creation and remain safe in Your loving hands. Creator, Defender, Healer, Abba, we praise Your for all You are doing in this. Restore lives and our economy and we who know it is all You offer our praise now. In Jesus, conquering name, in Your love Abba, and the Holy Spirit's guidance. Amen.

March 17, 2020

We are Yours

Let us fix our eyes on Jesus, the author and perfecter of our faith,
who for the joy you set before Him endured the cross, scorning its shame,
and sat down at the right hand of the throne of God. [1]

You, LORD, created us in Your image.
The image of You, the Triune God, the Three in One. [2]
Adam was created from the clay of Your perfect earth.
You gave Adam Your breath and made him a living soul. [3]
You made Adam's helpmate, Eve, from his rib. [4]
We, Your creation, are their descendants. We are clay and You are our potter.
Shape us according to Your will. We are all the work of Your hands. [5]

My heart says of You, "Seek His face!"
"Your face, LORD, I will seek." [6]
Moses said, "When you seek the LORD Your God,
You will find Him when you search for Him with all
Your heart and all your soul." [7]
Jeremiah said, "You, LORD, have good plans for us. Plans for our welfare
And not calamity to give us a future and a hope." [8]

"What then must we do?"
"You will call upon Me and come and pray to Me,
And I will listen to you. And you will seek Me and find Me,
When you search for Me with all your heart." [9]
"Ah, LORD God! Behold, You made the heaven and earth by Your great power
And by Your outstretched arm! Nothing is too difficult for You,
Who shows lovingkindness to thousands, but repays iniquity – " [10]

"When we call on You what will You do?"
"When you call to Me, and I will answer you, and I will tell you great
And mighty things, which you do not know." [11]
"When you pass through the waters, I will be with you;
And through the rivers, they will not overflow you.
When you walk through the fire, you will not be scorched,
Nor will the flame kindle upon you." [12]

"Do not be afraid, for I am with you; do not look anxiously about you,
For I am your God. I will strengthen you, surely, I will help you,
Surely I will uphold you with My righteous right hand." [13]
The righteous who run into it are saved." [14]
"He who dwells in the shelter of the Most High
Will abide in the shadow of the Almighty." [15]

"Oh, LORD, it is You who will deliver us from the snare of the trapper,
And from the deadly pestilence. It is You who will cover us with Your pinions,
And give us the refuge we seek under Your wings,
For Your faithfulness is our shield and bulwark.
Because of You, we will not be afraid of the terror by night,
Or the arrow that flies by day; of the pestilence that stalks in darkness,
Or the destruction that lays waste at noon." [16]

"Why, O LORD, would you do this for us?" we ask.
"You have revealed that our flesh is like grass
And our loveliness is like a flower.
And, at our breath we know that grass
Withers and flowers fade.
We can return to the dust LORD and be forgotten,
But Your word stands forever." [17]

"Because I love you, therefore I will deliver you.
I will set you securely on high because you have known My name.
You will call upon Me, and I will answer you,
I will be with you in trouble; I will rescue and honor you.
With a long life I will satisfy you, and let you behold My salvation." [18]
Praise Abba, "When my anxious thoughts multiply within me,
Your consolations delight my soul. [19]

"How can we describe You to those who don't know You yet?" God responds,
"I am the One who measured the waters in the hollow of My hand,
And marked off the heavens with the span of My outstretched arms.
It is I who calculated the dust of the earth in the measure,
And weighted the mountains out in a balance, and the hills in a pair of scales.
No one can direct or enlighten Me to new understanding. The foolish nations
And rulers are a drop from a bucket, a speck of dust on My scales." [20]

"I am the One who sits above the vault of the earth,
And sees its inhabitants as grasshoppers.
I have stretched out the heavens like a curtain
And have spread them out like a tent for My dwelling.
I am He who created the stars.
You cannot number the stars, but I call them by name.
And it is by My might that not one of them is missing." [21]

"My understanding and knowledge is inscrutable to you. [22]
My Beloved Son, Jesus, paid your debt and is your Intercessor with Me.
He loved you enough to die for you.
Turn to him now, for He is ready to receive you just as you are.
His relationship with you starts when you pray to Me for forgiveness.
My forgiveness is a free gift to you because Jesus paid your sin debt.
Why waste any more time? Unparalleled unity is yours." [23]

"We are prepared to give you strength when you are weary.
When you lack might, We will increase your power.
Even youths grow tired and weary and the old must reach out for support.
Vigorous youth stumble and the old cannot gain their feet,
But those who wait upon the LORD, they will gain strength; they will mount up
With wings like eagles, they will run and not get tired,
They will walk and not become weary." [24]

Jesus says, "Come unto Me, all you that labor and are heavy laden, and I will give you rest.
Take my yoke upon you and learn of Me; for I am meek and lowly in heart: and you shall find rest for your
Souls. For my yoke is easy, and my burden is light. [25]
"All authority has been given to Me in heaven and on earth.
Go therefore and make disciples of all nations, baptizing them in the name of the Father,
Son, and Holy Spirit, teaching them to observe all that I commanded you, and lo,
I am with you always, even to the end of the age." [26]

"Let not your heart be troubled; believe in God, believe also in Me.
In my Father's house are many dwellings places; if it were not so,
I would have told you; for I go to prepare a place for you.
And, if I go and prepare a place for you, I will come again, and receive you to Myself;
That where I am, there you may be also." Thomas asked, "How do we know the way to You?"
Jesus answered him. "I am the way, and the truth, and the life;
No one comes to the Father but through Me." [27]

"Peace I leave with you; My peace I give to you;
Not as the world gives, do I give to you.
Let not your heart be troubled, nor let it be fearful." [28]
"These things I have spoken to you, that My joy may be in you,
And that your joy may be made full.
This is My commandment that you love one another,
Just as I have loved you." [29]

"We believe in You, our Creator Abba, in Jesus the Son, and the Holy Spirit.
But there is a global threat to health, to life, to our economy.
What do we do now?"
"Rejoice in the LORD always; again, I say rejoice!
Let your gentle spirit be known to all men. The LORD is near.
Be anxious for nothing, but in everything by prayer and supplication
With thanksgiving let your request be made known to God." [30]

"Yes, Abba, we are praying, but the deadly virus is relentless."
"Let your requests be made known to Me. I am God.
And My peace, the peace of your Father God
which surpasses all comprehension shall guard your hearts
And minds in Christ Jesus." [31]
"Remember you can do all things through Me
Who strengthens you." [32]

"Abba, we are Your creation and You have placed eternity in our hearts." [33]
"I have not given you a spirit of fear, but of power, and of love and a sound mind." [34]
"We ask that You tame our fears. We believe. Help our unbelief." [35]
"We stand on the covenant You made with us through Christ Jesus." [36]
"We are Your beloved, and we cannot be snatched from Your hand." [37]
"What time we are afraid, we will trust in You, Your sovereignty." [38]
"You neither slumber nor sleep, nor do You become tired or weary." [39]

"What, then, will we say in response to these truths?"
"If God is for us, who can be against us? [40]
Who shall separate us from the love of Christ? shall tribulation, or distress, or persecution,
Or famine, or nakedness, or peril, or sword? Nay, in all these things we are more
Then conquerors through him that loved us. For I am persuaded, that neither death,
Nor life, nor angels, nor principalities, nor powers, nor things present, nor things to come,
Nor height, nor depth, nor any other creature, shall be able to separate
Us from the love of God, which is in Christ Jesus our LORD." [41]
"We will watch and wait expectantly for God who hears us.
You will not let our enemy (this virus) rejoice over us.
Though we fall, we will rise.
Though we live in darkness, You are our Light." [42]
"You are with us and mighty to save.
You will take great delight in us, and quiet us with your love,
And rejoice over us with singing." [43]

"We will delight ourselves in You LORD; and thank You for giving us
The desires of our hearts, (recovery from this virus). We will commit our way to You, LORD,
Trust also in You because we know You will do it." [44]
"We will be strong and courageous! We will not tremble or be dismayed,
For You, LORD, are with us at this time." [45]
"Even so, we will exult in You, Abba.
We will rejoice in You always, for You are the God of our salvation." [46]

Abba, Good Friday is only a few days away, but this piece wanted to be written and I could not deny it. Will there be another piece for Good Friday? I have a thought from Deuteronomy. Covid 19 is a burden for 2020 because it is bringing physical death to many, separating loved ones from family members in the hospital who are sick and those who die, die without loved ones with them, and our economy too is struggling to survive. Yet, I see You here in the midst of this with us. The Holy Spirit living inside of me shouts for me not to be afraid and to look for joy. Thank you for taming the fear that is trying to seed in my heart and mind. Thank you for giving me Your spirit of joy. I see and feel You Father and I am breathing You in. Make Your Presence felt at this time not just by Your beloved, but by all who will come to salvation through this pandemic. I know Your will is for all to be saved and I see the Holy Spirit reaching out to all needing salvation, and to all who are Your beloved. Bring the prodigals home and let those living lessor lives than is Your will for them recommit. I remember LORD Jesus that You prayed for me and all who be Yours at the Last Supper and I am grateful that Apostle John recorded it in John 17 for us, not just for a time like this but for all time. My prayer is gratitude and praise. By Your great power, undeserved mercy, and grace. Amen.

April 7, 2020

What God Seeks from Us
Call to Obedience

You shall not add or take away from the word I am commanding you. [1]
You will seek the LORD your God, and you will find Him,
If you search for Him with all your heart and all your soul. [2]
When you return to God (from your sinning), the LORD your God who is compassionate will not fail
You nor destroy you or forget the covenant with your fathers which He swore. [3]

Ten beneficial laws He gave us to show us how to live a better life now and please God forever.
You shall have no other gods before Me.
You shall not make idols, nor worship or serve them.
You shall not take the name of the LORD your God in vain.
Remember the Sabbath day, to keep it holy.
Honor your father and your mother.
You shall not murder.
You shall not commit adultery.
You shall not steal.
You shall not bear false witness against your neighbor.
You shall not covet. [4]

You shall love the LORD your God with all your heart, with all your soul, and all your might. [5]
You shall not follow other gods, any of the gods of the peoples who surround you. [6]
You shall not test God, but should diligently keep His commandments , testimonies, and His statues.
And you shall do what is right and good in the sight of the LORD that it may go well with you. [7]
He makes you know that man does not live by bread alone,
But man, lives by everything that proceeds out of the mouth of God. [8]
Remember the LORD your God, for it is He who is giving you power to make wealth
That He may confirm His covenant which He swore to your fathers. [9]
You shall love the LORD your God, and always keep His charge,
And His statutes, His ordinances, and commandments. [10]

If you listen obediently to my commandments to love the LORD your God
And serve Him with all your heart and all your soul,
God will give you rain in its season, grain, new wine, and oil.
Grass in your fields for your cattle, and you shall eat and be satisfied.
Beware, lest your hearts be deceived, and you turn away to serve and worship other gods.
Or the LORD's anger will kindle against you, and He will shut up the heavens, so there will be no rain And the
ground will not yield its fruit, and you will perish. [11]
Impress these words of God on your heart and on your soul;
Teach them to your sons, talking of them as you sit in your house and walk along the road
And when you lie down and rise up. Write them on your doorpost and on your gates,
So, your days and your sons days will be multiplied on the land
As long as the heavens remain above the earth.
Take care to keep all God's commandments to do it,
To love the LORD your God, to walk in all His ways and hold fast to Him,
Then the LORD will drive out nations before you, and dispossessed
Nations greater and mightier than you. [12]

Be careful to listen to all these commands, in order that it may be well with
You and your sons after you forever, for you will be doing what is good and right
In the sight of the LORD. Do not be ensnared to follow their practices and serve their gods
For God hates what they have done to serve their gods for they even burn their children to serve them. Do as
God commands you and be careful to not add nor take away from it. [13](12:28-32)
You shall not listen to the words of a false prophet, teacher,
Or a dreamer who directs you to serve other gods.
You shall follow the LORD your God and fear Him; and keep His commandments, listen to His voice, serve Him,
and cling to Him.[14] You shall surely tithe. [15]
You shall generously give to the poor and your heart shall not
Be grieved when you give to him,
Because of this thing the LORD your God will bless you
In all your work and in all your undertakings.[16]
Every man shall give as he is able, according to the blessing
Of the LORD which He has given you. [17]

You shall not distort justice; you shall not be partial, and you shall not take a bribe,
For a bribe blinds the eyes of the wise and perverts the words of the righteous.
Justice and only justice, you shall pursue, that you may live
And possess all the LORD gives you. [18]
Your leader shall keep a copy of the law and shall read it all the days of his life
That he may learn to fear God, by carefully observing all the words of this law
And these statues that his heart may not be lifted up above his countrymen and that
He may not turn aside from the commandment to the right or to the left. [19]

You shall not practice detestable things, sacrifice your children, practice
Divination, witchcraft, sorcery, or be a medium or spiritist, or call on the dead.
They have no place in your lives for you shall be blameless before God.
A woman shall not wear men's clothing, or a man women's clothing,
For this is an abomination to the LORD your God.[20]
Fathers shall not be punished for their sons, not the sons for their father,
But everyone for their own sin.
You shall not oppress a worker who is poor and needy whether a countryman or alien.
You shall not pervert the justice due an alien or an orphan,
Nor take a widow's garment in pledge. You shall remember
And care for the alien, and the orphan and for the widow in your midst. [21]

Moreover, the LORD your God will circumcise your heart and the heart of your descendants so love the
LORD your God with all your heart and with all your soul, in order that you may live. [22]
Then the LORD your God will prosper you abundantly in all the work of your hand, in your offspring,
Your animals and produce, for the LORD will again rejoice over your for good, just as
He rejoiced over your fathers; if you obey the LORD your God to keep
His commandments and His statues which are written in
The book of the law, if you turn to the LORD your God with all your heart and soul.
For this commandment which I command you today is not too difficult for you, nor is it out of reach.

But the word is very near you, in your mouth and in your heart,
That you may observe it. See, I have set before you today life and prosperity, and death and adversity; in That
I command you today to love the LORD your God, to walk in His ways and to keep
His commandments and His statues and His judgments, that you may live and multiply,
And that the LORD your God may bless you. [23]

Be strong and courageous, do not be afraid or tremble at them, for the LORD your God is the
One who goes with you. He will not fail you or forsake you. And the LORD is the one who goes ahead of you;
He will be with you. He will not fail you or forsake you. Do not fear or be dismayed." [24]
May the beloved of the LORD dwell in security by Him who shields him all day
And he dwells between His shoulders." [25]
There is none like the God of Jeshurun, who rides the heavens to your help,
And through the skies in His majesty. Blessed are you, O Israel; who is like you, a people
Saved by the LORD, who is the shield of your help, and the sword of your majesty!
So, your enemies shall cringe before you, and you shall tread upon their high places. [26]

Abba, Moses had so much to remind Israel of before they entered the Promised Land. No one can read Deuteronomy and say that You did not give them all they needed to know to live faithfully and in Your will. These were not hard or unreasonable rules, but rules to give them life and to protect them from the enemies surrounding them. Yet, even when they failed and fell away from all Your wisdom and unfailing guidance and You punished them, You allowed them to confess their sin and return to Your sheepfold. I know as You are sovereign and unchanging that these rules apply to us in America. I know You can still protect us from our enemies, even the enemies of illness and death. Thank you for being with this in this time of Covid 19. Thank you for giving these rules of life and always loving not just the descendants of Abraham, but us who were chosen to be blessed through Abraham. Great Holy Father, love without end. Amen.

April 15, 2020

Eternal Beings Created in Love

Abba, You created the whole universe for mankind who You created out of agape love.
Our world, a tiny planet in the vastness with a perfect garden home was spoken into being.
Created by your own hand Father Adam and Mother Eve breathed.
There in the garden there was harmony between nature, beast, man, and You.
Satan crept in with lies and Adam and Eve disobeyed, so sin marred them.
Their lives could never be the same, so they lost their innocence and garden home.
They lost their unique relationship and fellowship with You.

Sin was now a part of them and passed down through all their kin.
They now were separated from You and struggled to do all You would have done for them.
Cain killed his brother Abel out of jealousy and his blood marred the earth.
Cain's descendants followed in his legacy, but You raised up a family though his brother Seth.
The fallen world in time You destroyed through the great flood and started over new.
Through Noah and his wife, their three sons and daughters-in-law, mankind filled the earth again.
Sin remained in their members and continued to strangle and restrain nature from Your plan.

Abba, I don't need to tell You the story of Your chosen son Abraham and his wife Sarah.
Nor the story of his descendants who came to be called Israelites.
I will praise You that Your son, Jesus, came to redeem them and those of us called Gentiles.
Jesus out of great love and compassion, the perfect holy sacrifice, died to free all mankind of sin.
Yes, redemption was made available to all and forced on none.
Once accepted, salvation frees us from the penalty of sin but does not stop us from choosing to sin.
Obedience in love is all God asks of us and we sojourn on our planet home.

Some argue there is no God that the universe arose by accident and not Your design.
They believe there is birth and death and nothingness for us, Your creation.
Abba, I know by Your word that we were created for far more than this existence.
In the heart of each of us, is the desire for eternal life without pain or death.
You placed this in our hearts along with our longing to find dependency and wholeness in You.
Satan and sin in our lives make us struggle for independence and self-sufficiency.
Satan would rob us of the freedom and blessings You offer to all You redeem.

My heart longs for Your presence because in it there is eternal security and peace.
Mankind is Your creation, and You seek us out to redeem our souls.
You look at the condition of our hearts and our thoughts, not our bodies.
No, You don't look at us by color, culture, or economic value.
How sad it must make You that we look to the outside and judge so unfairly.
You see us as eternal beings living in temporary vessels that You created to be with You.
Creatures You will one day judge to decide where we will spend eternity.

Abba forgive us for being so unkind to one another for You have called us to love.
You have called us to serve one another in Your name.
We repeat the mistakes of the past and relive instead of forgiving them.
We build up walls around us and live in fear inside of them.
We hold back love and trust sometimes even from those we call family or friends.
Surely the news tells us this is no way to live.
Forgive us and bring healing, Abba. Bring wholeness in You.

Once saved, we are eternal beings who will one day live on a restored earth.
From the day our first parents disobeyed in the garden this was Your plan.
Clearly being restored is what we all must seek and can find in Christ.
Oh, the evil heart of men and women who will forgo it for the temporary pleasures of life.
I passionately protest evil in our world and ask You rebuke it.
Sadly, I know the hearts of many will continue to pursue the world and not You.
Abba, I have read Revelation and know Your plan is in progress to restore all creation.

I know there is a new heaven and earth being prepared.
I also know the peril and tribulation for all who do not find You now.
The world is in the final stage of labor, and we must live in it still.
Let the Holy Spirit reach the hearts of those who are not yet Yours.
Save them for Yourself for I know this is Your will for them.
Eternity is in the heart of every man and woman but where they live it, they must choose.
For me, the only choice is Your presence for all eternity.

Abba, the world's struggle is clear. Racism spoils and defiles the hearts of many. It was never Your desire for us. The virus sucks the breath from the young and old alike throughout the entire planet. War and genocide, disease, accidents, disasters, starvation, and dehydration kill each day. Some party on and ignore the warning signs of Your displeasure with Your creation. So, it was during Bible times.

Abba forgive us and be patient still. Continue to be with Your children. If Grandma Weidner were here, she'd say, "Jesus has to be coming, soon." She would be right. I am afraid for those who are lost. You won't make them choose salvation, and the saved cannot force them to choose You either. I know You would want heaven to be crowded, and so do I, but I know it won't be.

How sad, Abba, You had a plan to restore mankind before You created Adam and Eve. Jesus fulfilled and paid for the plan. The Holy Spirit is in the hearts of all who chose You, yet there are so many not living in You. I am overwhelmed but offer praise because You are sovereign and not overwhelmed. Abba, I love You, forever Your grateful daughter. Amen.

July 16, 2020

Chapter Four

The Trinity Calling

I think these pieces come from the heart of the Trinity to us.
Take a moment and listen and breathe Them in.

Love Letter from Jesus

Dearest Child,

Before the world was created, I shared glory with My Father. I looked ahead in time and saw you and instantly loved you. Loving you We had a plan to give you a future and hope. I left heaven for you and sojourned on the earth. Opened my arms and died to bring you salvation.

I have been watching you, ever so patiently. The path you have selected disappoints me. It will lead to Me, but it is strewed with hazards and barriers that you must face alone for you have not asked me to journey beside you.

I call you to Me now. Just ahead there is a fork in the path. Choose the path where I wait and allow me to journey beside you. For on this path, I will never leave you, and I will help you deal with all the consequences of your former choices.

You have a strong spiritual heritage to lean on. Just last week, your Grandma Agnes thanked me for all her family here and there. She asked for those of you who have not yet finished the journey to My Father's throne. She asked about all her grandchildren, great-grandchildren, and the wee great–great-grandchildren for all you are some much closer to the end of life's journey then when she left you. Time is always joyous here, but nothing compares to Homecoming celebrations and Heaven won't be complete for her until you all join us here.

Although I do not journey with you now, I am not ignorant how you spend your time, your money, and how you care for your body. I know the world's influence is great on you, but I overcame the world. Come to Me and I will cleanse My temple and supper with you. Then, the world will see you as I planned, and you will influence the world for Me.

Do not be deceived by the lies of my enemy. His plans are to destroy you and to take joy in your separation from Me. Fall back to the simple trust of childhood. Trust in Me and I will give you My strength, My Joy, My Power, My Confidence and My Love. You cannot find these things in the world for I am not there. Look inside your heart for I stand there in full armor to overcome the evil one to redeem you for Myself. Fall back and I will take you under My wings to shield you once again.

Yet, a little while and your journey will end. Come to Me now, so I may finish it with you and stand beside you at My Father's throne.

Loving you always,

Jesus

Unconditional Forgiveness

God forgives unconditionally.
Satan reminds us unmercifully.
What are you going to accept?

God always hears the sinner's prayer,
And forgives His newly adopted child.
God always hears His child's sincere prayer of confession.
Then forgives and forgets.
*"As far as the east is from the west,
So far has He removed your transgressions."* [1]

Satan, the Father of lies and deception,
Cannot resurrect the sin or undo the unconditional forgiveness.
He can only deny it happened by casting doubts into your heart.

So, then rebuke Satan in Christ's power and see him flee.
"Satan, you are lying.
I gave my sin to God, and He forgave me
And He remembers it no more.
I remember it now only to praise Him,
And to remind me that no sin has enough value
To draw me away from God.
I rebuke you in the name of Jesus."

Satan cannot take you from Christ's loving hands.
He doesn't have that kind of power.
In fact, Satan has no power in your life as one of Christ's elect,
Except what you foolishly allow.

Stand up to Demons of Doubt.
Rebuke Satan, claim the victory, and praise God.
***"Peace, I leave with you;
My peace I give to you;
Not as the world gives, do I give you.
Let not your heart be troubled, nor let it be fearful."*** [2]
Let this be your certificate of confirmation
That God has forgiven you.
You are His, you asked, He gave,
And it is settled evermore.

From God to my mind to your heart – Peace.

March 23, 2003

I Know You

I know who you've become.
It's no surprise, but it saddens Me.
Still, I love you unconditionally.

I know who you'll become.
It could surprise you, oh but not Me.
Turn your life over to Me, I've special plans for you to see.

Your friends don't know Me, so I am not with them.
You cannot find Me in food, or drink, or drugs.
My dearest child, I know your loneliness, I'll heal you with My love.

Don't look for me in material things.
I am not into things, so you can't find Me on Etsy or eBay.
Search for Me now with all your heart, I am nearby today.

Your choice is to delay but only Satan wins that way.
You suffer without Me child, so does your family.
Someday another family might suffer too, it's for you to choose this day.

I love you just as you are, for you were made without mistake.
My Son died for you, so do not delay.
Come back to Us today.

Satan's lies are meant only to lead you further astray.
There is a future full of life following Me.
So much sadness if you continue your own way.

My plans are to give you a future and hope, a life of purpose.
Come now just as you are.
Take my hand, you are so beautiful in Us.

God
October 3, 2004

Dearest Son,

I knew you before you were born.
Before your mother was even married,
She thought about the children she might have.
It was then that I whispered your name, Jared Scott,
In her ear and she took it to heart.

It was in her heart's eye she first saw you,
Not as an infant, but as the remarkable
Blue eyed, blonde haired child you would become.
As your special gift, I allowed you a quick sense of humor.
It's a fine thing to make others laugh with you.

I bestowed on you the love of animals,
A heart more loving than you pretend,
And I allowed you the time
To develop a special bond of love with Little Dar.
She, by the way, loves you still and is so immensely proud of you.
And don't doubt how much your other grandparents love you.

So sure, of who you were your mom opened
A saving account in your name,
When you had three months left to knit in her womb.
She had a mother's heart of love for you even then,
And her arms ached to hold you
And to breathe in your baby sweetness.

You gave Me my special required place in your heart
On September 1, 1985
I watched as you entered the waters of baptism.
Watched as you joined My beloved son, Jesus, in his
Death, burial, and resurrection.
I was pleased then to call you My beloved son, Jared Scott.

I've always known you, and I've been pleased when
You included me in your life's choices.
I'm always glad to hear from you – a please Father here,
And a thank you Father there.
When you're ready I'll be happy to see you in My house again.
You understand – I know you'll be back.

Always,
Your loving Father

Come to Me

"Come to Me just as you are.
I can see that you are weary and unable to carry
Your burdens alone. I want to give you rest.[1]

You are My child and I have planned
Peace for you, not as the world gives,
Only as I can give.[2]

If you wait on Me, I will renew your strength.
Then, you will mount up with wings like eagles.
To run without tiring and to walk and not get weary.[3]

I will be with you as you pass through the waters
And not even the rivers will be allowed to overflow you.
Fires will not scorch you and no flame will kindle upon you.[4]

You allowed Me into your life as Savior and friend.
You cannot be snatched from My hand.
Remember you are not of this world.[5]

I prayed for you the night before My crucifixion.
So, let not your heart be troubled, neither let it be afraid.
I intercede for you now with the Father.[6]

I am always ready for you to cast your
Burdens upon Me, for I carried you to the cross.
Place your trust in Me now, and I will rescue you.[7]

I am your refuge and strength,
A very present help in trouble.
I am always with you even to the end of the world."[8]

Your Savior and Friend,
Jesus

April 6, 2008

A Message

America the Beautiful God could have spared you. But did not, why not?
Have Hope

Men of great spiritual faith looking for religious freedom for all founded our country.
They said, "in God we trust."
Every aspect of their faith was revealed in both their personal and professional lives.
Against incredible odds, we won the Revolutionary War.

Now men of America say, not based on the Declaration of Independence
Or the Constitution, "let us separate the church from the state."
Let us remove God from our state motto and coin,
So, we do not offend those who do not believe, as did our founding fathers.

God gave each of us freedom of will. So, we can choose to believe in Him or not,
So, we can practice good or evil.
Free will chose evil on September 11, 2001, piercing our country,
our hearts in a way never before imagined.
Now we call for justice, and if more innocents are hurt,
We will not call them victims, but "collateral damage."

America the Beautiful, God chose you,
Because of the faith of those who came to these shores looking for religious freedom.
You were His elect and by His blessings you became the greatest nation on earth.
Look to Him now. Turn your minds and hearts to Him not because of our national tragedy,
Or fear of further terrorism, or retribution.

But, because God says to us, **"Turn to Me and make yourself right with Me, and I will heal your land."**
God was not surprised by the events that scar our land and our hearts.
Return now to the God who cleanses, who comforts, and has a plan to restore us.
His word reveals, "If God is for us, who can be against us."
America the Beautiful, God still is God, and loves you still.

September 16, 2001

Obey Beloved

Kneel down and surrender to the Holy Spirit.
Listen and obey the Spirit's call.
Turn your heart to the sound of thunder.
God whispers tender words of love.

We are called to be His people.
Obey all that He commands.
Fall down and seek forgiveness.
Boundless love waits.

Bring your broken lives, broken bodies, and broken spirits.
Lay all your brokenness at His feet.
Rise us, rise up Beloved and worship at His throne.
Leave your brokenness behind.

Stand up Beloved and reflect His glory.
Be strong for you are no longer your own.
Go forth beloved to the fields white unto harvest.
Gather in the lost until the job is done.

Live for Him and praise Him each day.
Return to Him when your sojourn ends.
Kneel beloved and cast your crowns at His feet.
Arise, beloved, and enjoy Eternity with Him.

August 8, 2010, bulletin draft
November 30, 2015

Forgiveness is Letting Go

Abba, Charles Dickens' character Marley in a <u>Christmas Carol</u>
Is seen carrying a long chain forged from his misdeeds.
Dickens easily could have written in a character or two who
Carried rotting corpses on their backs.
Individuals who carried those about who they would not forgive.

Abba, You are well aware of those of whom I speak. Unforgiving Christians, forbid!
They cling to anger and bitterness and wear the perfume of nobility.
Yes, they may have been slighted, misjudged, misunderstood, and perhaps even neglected.
So, isn't it their right to harbor ill feelings and thoughts of ill-will?
Oh, <u>yes, it is their right</u> – to fan the flames of heartbreak and disease in their own bodies.

Abba, how many really were truly wronged?
How many took something small and made it large?
How many judged another culpable when circumstances
Were truly outside their control?
How many heard, "I'm sorry," and chose to hold a grudge?

You, Abba, forgave Adam and Eve their sin of disobedience in the garden.
You clothed them and removed them from their garden home
To prevent them from living their eternal lives in sin.
Yet, You did not require them to forfeit their lives.
You didn't start mankind over with a couple who would remain obedient to You.

Jesus modeled and taught forgiveness all during His ministry among us.
He told Peter that forgiveness was unlimited in His answer to forgive seventy times seven. [1]
Jesus from His cross forgave those crucifying Him. Can anything be more unforgivable?
"Forgive them for they know not what they do." [2] He forgave us too for His sacrifice was for us!
So, why is it so hard for those I love to forgive me for far less?

Truly, I always tried to give my best to all and to be there when they called.
You know my heart and that I'd never deliberately cause anyone heartache or pain.
Yet, You know too that I am human and make mistakes.
Is there no omission, delay, slip, or mistake defendable?
Why am I <u>not loved</u> enough by them to be accepted for the <u>sum</u> of who I am?

I don't believe that anything I have done is unforgivable.
You taught me that I am worthy of love, acceptance, and forgiveness.
My love for them remains unchanged and I forgive the pain of their unforgiveness.
With Jesus I say, **"Father, don't hold this against them."** [3]
Love them, Abba. Bring them the healing they need. Remove my corpse from their backs.

October 8, 2019

Abba, I have been working on this for several days, but I've been trying to understand it far longer. Should I just be grateful that only two people refuse to forgive me? One charge, LORD, You know was nothing within my control or done with my permission. The other was simply a phone call notification that I didn't make sooner. Was it really wrong for me to rest after seventeen days of stress as I cared for Mom during her last hospital stay and hospice? Why was it only my burden alone to shoulder? Why did he not stay in touch with me?

For the other I simply don't understand the charges cited or even know what has been held back. If I don't understand how can I make amends? Why has a barrier been erected against me, yet money and gifts are received from me with little or no thanks? Is it because they can't blame the dead or others they disregard?

My son says, I need to accept their judgment without defense, without being able to talk it out, to make amends, to restore our relationships. Judgment isn't the same as justice. Only You have the right to judge me, to punish me, and truly I feel that justice from You holds no judgment. Judge me, Abba, for I trust Your judgment and justice above theirs. You love me unconditionally and will let no one separate me from You.

This is my prayer, Abba, please heal their hurts. Rebuke Satan or his minions from using this breach as a weapon against them. Restore their souls and spirits towards You because in You we can have unity again. I fear as each day passes their scars grow. Restore me to them for You alone have this power. You desire unity in the family and Satan wants only to destroy it. So, I know the answer to this prayer is in Your will. I know it is best for them and I won't let them go. You created me to love them and as Your love won't let them go, neither will I. Family is what You desire for Your creation and in this I will trust.

Two more prayers today that aren't a part of this prose. It has been thirty-nine years since Daddy went home. Let him know I still miss him and the relationship we would have had as adults. Let him know that his six great-grandchildren are doing well. Give my love to him and all mine gathered there with You. Be with Darlene today and let this testing reveal no cancer, then allow our focus to be back with her lung that is still suspicious. I love You. Forever Abba, Jesus, and the Holy Spirit. Amen.

2021 One person has been restored to me. Thank you, Abba, for I believe I gained this through having a covenant prayer partner. She is praying now for the other person. Thank you for the healing that will come to him. Amen.

2022 Thank you, Abba, for restoring unity with him too.

"You Are Not a Plastic Christian."

"I knew you before your first heartbeat. I placed within your heart a sacred place for Me to dwell but gave you freewill to fill it with My Spirit, fill it with useless temporary earthly things, or leave it void. I was so pleased when you chose Me, and the angels in heaven rejoiced as My Spirit filled the void and sealed you for eternity. You were made new that day. Your sins were forgiven and forgotten, but I did not take away your freewill, so you must constantly choose to grow in Me, and trust my love for you even when living in Me isn't easy."

"You are not a plastic Christian."

"I did not reshape you into perfection or make you into a puppet whose strings I control. I will not force your legs to walk with Me, your arms or hands to serve me, program your brain to hear or listen to me, and I won't force your mouth to speak of Me or to Me. I placed the desire for these things in your heart, but you must choose to serve and worship Me."

A Accept that salvation in you is complete, and nothing or no one has the power to take it from you.

S Surrender to My power and my plan for your life.

K Keep praying unceasingly for I hear all your prayers and collect your tears in My bottle.

"You are not a plastic Christian."

"I will never fail or leave you. Just as I am real, our enemy, Satan is real. He will lie to you! His lies are fiery darts meant to bring you pain, break your trust in Me, and rob you of your joy. His demons whisper lies and want you to believe that. 'You aren't good enough;' 'You aren't smart enough;' 'You are unworthy of love;' 'You can't measure up;' 'You'll always fail;' 'You are not acceptable the way you are;' and, My child he will tell you; 'You have to earn your relationship with Me.'"

"Fiery darts try to burrow into your mind and heart and push Me away. Lies have no place in you for this is where I abide. You, My child, were created by Me and what I create is good. Your beauty to Me is more than man can measure. Even when youth loosens its grip on you, your temporary body fails, your beauty will remain. I don't see wrinkles or scars as ugly marks on your body, but evidence of your walk and reliance on Me."

" Don't confuse your need to grow and learn with imperfection or failure. Again, I did not simply download you with all the talents and skills you will come to use, but I put the capacity for all you will be within your reach, but you must reach for them, practice them, and yes, beloved, give them back to Me."

"You are not a plastic Christian."

"Jesus, My Only Son, did not spare Himself the agony of the cross. He is your advocate with Me. Since He died for you, He will spare nothing for you. Troubles are natural to this life. My Spirit will be with you when you are distressed. Never give up, for I will give you My power. March on, My Child, with courage. Look up to Me! Look for the joy in each day! My right hand upholds you!"

"Jesus is your Good Shepherd. He is the Guardian of your soul. We, beloved, neither slumber nor sleep. We go beside you. We will direct your steps and delight in the details of your life as you eagerly follow where We lead. You may stumble, be bruised, be bloodied; you may be broken, but never lost to Us. We will hide you in the shelter of Our presence. We will pick you up and carry you, and you will heal."

"You, beloved child, will grow stronger each time you pass through deep waters for you will feel Us with you, rivers of water will not sweep you away as you hold onto Us, you will walk through fires of hardship and know that We are with you, and so long as you abide in Us, the enemies' fiery darts will not kindle upon your beloved head. (Isaiah 43:2) Take my hand beloved, I will lead you on the best pathways through your life and bring you home at your journey's end."

"You are not a plastic Christian."

"I want to lavish My love on you, beloved, for you are special to me. Oh, I know the times you live in and how turbulent the news. Pray, beloved, about it all and see the shield of My love before you. I will take your suffering and turn it to good, give you beauty for ashes, wipe away your tears, and give you joy in the morning. Since you are Mine and I love you, no one can ever be against you and succeed."

"No one can snatch you from My hand. I paid for you with the precious blood of Jesus, and He overcame hell and death. Eternity is real and doesn't last a lifetime, but for all time. There you will see all that has been prepared for you, for all the beloved children of My Son."

"You are not a plastic Christian."

"Give Me all your cares and burdens. You are My child, My beloved, and I never want you to carry them. I will give you rest from them, but only so long as you don't take them back. I delight in you each day as you trust me to keep all the promises I've made to you. Nothing is too hard for me. I created the universe and you. I call the stars by name and have not lost one of them."

"I know your name and have planned a place for you in heaven. There, when your life's journey ends, and you finally come home, all your pain, burdens, crying, and sadness will melt away with your former life, and death will not stalk your glorified body, for death has lost its stings inside the vast gates of Eternity."

"You are not a plastic Christian."

"You beloved are My child and I made you a living creature with freewill and a capacity to be all I've planned for you to be. You are a living breathing creature wonderfully and uniquely made. I want you to be you, so don't disguise yourself as anybody else. I see and love you as you are, and more, beloved, as you will be. Put on My living armor, trust My heart for you, and I will see you through to eternity where you will live forever with Us. I'm very proud of you."

Love always, Abba

Looking Back to See Ahead

Earth shattered by the impact! Estrangement! Loss to all mankind!
Eden was perfect – your eternal garden home of beauty and delight.
The animals called into being were peaceful and may have spoken.
You, Adam and Eve, were the greatest of God's living creations.
You were created by Father God's own hands in the image of the Trinity.
With God's own breath He made you living souls, created to delight and serve Him.
You were made for each other, two yet one, and walked daily with our Creator.

My first parents, you were created in sinless perfection to share love in the Trinity.
You were not created slaves or puppets but created with freewill each.
Father and Mother, you were given dominion over your garden home and all its creatures.
You did not plant the garden but could savor all its fruits save one.
Was this obedience then too much to ask for all Father God had given you?
Just of one tree you could not taste, but its beauty was yours to see.
The Tree of the Knowledge of Good and Evil was not yours for good reason.

How is it that you shared such intimacy with the Creator?
In Eden, you could walk with Him, look into His eyes, and speak to Him face to face.
Love, you shared love with Him without concern or fear!
How then did you listen to another voice, not His?
Serpents were not strange to you in Eden as they walked about.
Oh, but one came to you, and you did listen to his lies.
Boldly he asked, *"Did God really say, 'You must not eat of any tree in the garden?'"*

Eve you answered him truthfully, "We may eat from all save one.
Father God said, 'Do not touch that tree for then you will surely die!'"
That crafty serpent then contradicted your Creator with a promise and a lie.
"No, not die, but be like Him, knowing good and evil."
His words of doubt and distrust were no doubt new to your innocent minds.
"Oh, Eve, why did you trust and not doubt <u>his</u> words?
Whatever did he do for you? Did you ever feel any kind of love from him?

Oh, Mother Eve, why did you not wait for the cool of the day when God would come to you?
Your words could have been, "Wait, I will ask Abba when He comes?"
No, you took your eyes off of Abba and looked favorably on the forbidden fruit.
You ate it and Adam who was with you ate it too.
Oh, Father Adam why did you not stop her and order the serpent away?
Yes, your eyes were opened, and you were ashamed of your disobedience and hid your nakedness.
You were now afraid of the One who created and cared for you.

Dear parents, you opened the door to sin that day by letting doubt come in.
Yes, words of doubt spoken from the father of lies, seeded in your minds.
Distrust of your loving Creator then took root, and you did not seek Him.
Did He ever lie to you? No! Your distrust of Him led you to think of eating the pretty fruit.
Did you really need to disrupt your beautiful lives to know good and evil?
You knew agape love in our Abba, why wasn't that all you needed to know?

No, your focus turned inward, and you discounted all you already had and the required punishment.
Sin entered Eden through you, and you could not stay and eat from the Tree of Life.
God sacrificed two animals to make coverings for your nakedness.
Their blood was spilled because of your sin and mortality, death, became your lot.
Then you were cast from Eden and a cherubim with a flaming sword barred the way back in.
How sad because Father God also placed a curse on each of you which became our legacy.
Dear parents, your sin and curses became ours even before we were born.
Yes, you are both to blame, but I can claim no innocence.

My life unlike yours was after the cross of Calvary.
I have my Savior Jesus for my advocate with Abba.
I know we have an enemy who would accuse us before our most Holy Father.
Yes, I know, Satan and his followers still speak lies.
They would speak of doubt, fear to us, and encourage us to distrust God.
Ah, but what a lesson I did learn from both of you.
I will keep my eyes on Abba and not look at the pretty fruits.

I will speak to Abba and the Son and seek guidance from the Holy Spirit.
I will ask that They rebuke my enemies defending me against their lies.
When I am hurt, bruised, bloodied, or broken by life, I will remember Them.
I will remember my Loving Creator, my Redeemer, and the Holy Spirit living inside of me.
I will ask Them to clean and cleanse my mind of all doubt, distrust, and fear.
I will stay true and focused on Their promises of good here and eternal life in Heaven.
I will wait and watch expectantly for Eden to be restored and greet Them there.

February 5, 2020, Happy Birthday, David

Abba, the title came to me in my sleep last night, and I stirred and wrote it on a tissue box so I would remember it. Thoughts of how my first parents were deceived have been with me for several days, for I too hear whispered lies that speak words of distrust, doubt, and fear. Did they learn the lesson that has now come to me from the Holy Spirit, and not repeat their mistake? My list of who to meet in heaven grows. Abba, surely, Adam and Eve are there welcoming home to Eden all their children who believe and have not been deceived. Thank you, Jesus for advocating for me with Abba and thank you Holy Spirit for being my guide home. Surely, Eden beckons me. Thank you, Father, that my name is in the book called Life and I cannot be snatched from Your hands. Forever and ever. My love for the Trinity, One in Three. Amen.

Their Steadfast Love
No greater love than this!

Loss, tragedy, and pain are hallmarks of humanity.
It comes without warning at times.
Or it lingers long tormenting us.
It attacks the core of our being.
We are made raw with our tears.
Yet our tears offer no relief.

Bruised, bloodied, and broken we seek healing.
When it fails to come, we get stuck and wallow in our misery.
Our grief is unique to us, and we feel lost and alone.
We hold our misery close, turning away from the proffered comfort of others.
They may share in our loss, but their grief is not equal to our own.
If allowed bitterness creeps in to rob us of any joy.

Satan whispers lies from the darkness to crush us in our fragileness.
We cry out to God and hear only deafening silence from Him.
Our prayers and tears ask "why" but we are not answered.
We ask why as His children; our experience is less regarded than others.
We doubt His love, His goodness, maybe even His existence.
We ask ourselves, "Were we foolish to ever believe and trust Him?"

Then God speaks and reminds us.
"Beloved children, have you forgotten that I have good plans for you.
I created the universe to give you an amazing home.
Come to Me and leave your burdens at my throne.
Here I will wipe away your tears and comfort you in My outstretched arms.
You are not ever alone. My son, Jesus, sits with me and advocates for you.
My Holy Spirit dwells inside of you and remains your guide."

Jesus speaks to give us new understanding,
"I will speak to loss, tragedy, and pain.
I left heaven, My Father, and the Holy Spirit to sojourn on earth with you.
In human form from helpless infant to man I remained.
Royal earthy parents raised me. Dear Mother Mary and Father, Joseph.
I knew human life without the same unity of the Trinity I once shared.
I dealt with all you did and more for I was still divine."

"Yes, I fed you, healed your diseases, restored your frames, and raised the dead.
I was obedient to the Father and our plan to restore mankind.
I had a family; I loved in human terms; I ate; I breathed; I worked; I lived!
I called twelve to be My disciples and gave them healing powers.
Many believed in Me, followed Me, but none of them understood Our plan.
I lived knowing Roman crucifixion would end my earthly mission."

"I let My calloused carpenter's wrists be pierced with crude spikes.
I rode the saddle of the cross with yet another spike piercing through My feet.
I forced My flogged and bleeding back against the coarseness of the cross for hours.
Raised myself up against the spikes in my wrists and feet to catch a faint breath.
I hung naked upon a criminal's cross, guiltless of any sin of My own.
My beard plucked out, my bruised and pain ridden body seeped blood from open wounds."

"My followers deserted Me in fear. My tormentors mocked, cursed, and spat upon Me.
My garments were divided as the prophets foretold, one won through the casting of lots.
A crown of thorns pierced my bloodied brow.
Sweat, tears and blood clouded the remaining vision of my blackened eyes.
I knew human suffering as no other ever crucified for I was betrayed by one of My own.
I suffered the weight of all sin, never having sinned."

"Betrayed too by the religious leaders who knew the scriptures pointing to My coming.
Falsely tried, I was found innocent yet condemned by Pilate.
Flogged, humiliated, mocked, bruised, bloodied and swollen, I thirsted.
Through my wounds muscle and organs could be seen.
Pain screamed from My flesh and every fiber of my torn body.
If physical pain was not enough, now I knew the ugliness of sin in My dying members."

"More was required than the body and mind could offer for the cost of mankind's salvation.
No beloved, I suffered in spirit too.
The Father and the Spirit withdrew from Me, not because of My agony but from sin.
Remember Divine Holiness must always remain separated from sin.
I didn't feel alone, abandoned, and hopeless.
For this space of time, I was alone, abandoned, and hopeless carrying your sins."

"All those hours of pain trying to breathe and being thirsty not just for water but for you.
This was the only time since before the world began, I was without the Father and the Spirit.
I was no longer a member of the unity of the Trinity for all mankind.
The agony of separation tore My heart, My divine, and human spirit.
I was away from heaven on sinful earth, the last closeness of the Divine was no longer mine.
I was obedient to the Father and was dying in human flesh for mankind and could not feel Them."

"My agony from this loss can still be read, '*My God, My God, why have You forsaken Me?*'
Yes, I cried out to Abba, and He did not answer Me.
Even so, I did not forget from whence I came and whence I was going.
My last thoughts were of you, '*Father forgive them for they know not what they do!*'
Then, finishing all that was required I gave up my life, '*Father into Your hands I commit My Spirit.*'
No bone in My body was broken, as foretold, but a Roman spear did pierce My side."

"My beloved child, I did all of this for you.
So, in your loss, tragedy and pain, in your bleakest hours, I will never leave you.
We hear your cries, gather up your tears, and offer solace only We can give.
Look up to our thrones with praise and gather with Us there.
The crown of thorns meant to mock became My Victor's crown.
Yes, on the third day after My crucifixion Abba raised Me from among the dead."

"I conquered sin and death beloved and was raised again to unity in the Trinity.
Rejoice beloved even in your loss, your tragedy, and pain.
For as it was in the beginning so it will be in the end.
The world Father God created is without end and will be restored again.
Here you will live with us in a restored earth never to suffer again.
You and yours, all who believe and remain faithful will see rewards."

"You and Yours will have all the delights of your eternal life and all the joys of heaven.
No, you are never alone because the Holy Spirit is ever with you.
Father God does hear all your prayers and answers from His sovereign will.
When you are hurting and don't feel Us, continue to believe.
The Father once answered 'No' to My earnest prayer to avoid the suffering of the cross.
He said, 'No,' beloved, so We could offer you heaven for all eternity."

August 24, 2020

Abba, I heard You say mankind doesn't understand what loss, tragedy, and pain can really entail. We want to be an exception to what people's daily face on this sin spoiled earth. You reminded me of Your Son, Jesus, and all He gave up for Me. How He lived His whole life in the shadow of the cross. Day by day He knew what was in the offering, but thankfully I did not. You know I visit His suffering especially come the time we call Easter and yet I still do not understand or appreciate His cruel handling and suffering. Even now I see Mary with her mother's heart, gently removing the crown of thorns from her firstborn son's forehead and washing the blood away with her tears.

Abba, I know from this side of the cross what Mary didn't understand. Abba Father, Precious Jesus, and Holy spirit thank you for the plan of my redemption. Jesus' blood cleansed me from all my trespasses and sins. He clothed me with His righteousness and someday, Abba, I will lay crowns at His scarred feet. Help me, Father, to have as many as I might. I remember to look up and hold on even now when I get overwhelmed by life. I will finish my course soon and live forever in Heaven because of the completed work of Jesus on the cross. Your acceptance, Abba, marks my debt paid in full. And the Holy Spirit abides in me and will see me forever home. All glory and honor Holy Trinity. Your world without end, Amen.

Color

Abba, the world seems to have gone mad over color.
Yet, I am grateful that You didn't create our world in just
Black and white or even shades of gray.
I enjoy the colors of the world with all the various shades and hues.
Crayons when I was child were a box of eight, now at least twenty-eight.

Color clearly means a lot to You for You created the world in all the colors I plainly see.
I walk through conservatories and aviaries and see just a glimpse of what Your world has to offer.
I do love the variety of colors created in plants, trees, flowers, and leaves.
Yet, when I see animals, I am not surprised at what You do with just black, white, and red.
So, why should your greatest creation, mankind, not share in the same variations?

I look at the birds that come to my Ohio backyard feeders and no two are alike.
I have a pair of cardinals that come to visit, and the male is red and bright.
But I am drawn to the female in muted tones of brown with soft undertones of red.
The starlings are mostly black but somehow reflect light and are iridescent blue.
The finches are brown with red throats and red peeks out through their folded wings.

The grackles too are black and light reflects iridescent blue from just their heads.
The sparrows are all browns and black and I see no common pattern in them.
The mourning doves are quite beautiful in shades of tan and gray.
I've seen a woodsy woodpecker or two and admire the white woven against the black.
And, just once a hawk graced John's fir tree majestic in his blend of muted colors.

Now I like to visit zoos because the animals there reflect more of the variety in the world.
I've seen so many colors in elephants, giraffes, gorillas, baboons, and hippopotamuses.
Oh, but wait what of black bears, brown bears, polar bears, lions, tigers, and panda bears?
What of the soft grays, browns, and shades of white in kangaroos and their baby joeys?
How many colors could I count in monkeys? And are orangutans red or orange?

Now zebras are a favorite of mine for they are black, white, and still no two are alike.
In my yard a few squirrels come to eat and play, and I will concede the white ones are my favorite.
A pair of white squirrels once lived in our attic before they left, and the soffit was repaired.
John used to call them "my buddies" whenever he saw them when we were together.
Yet, I never once noticed they were concerned over their color or the lack thereof.

So, Abba, why does color mean so much to the humans of Your creation?
You created just two humans, a single pair with the genetic code for all mankind.
When You destroyed the world by flood and left only eight humans alive,
Wasn't all the colors of mankind present in those precious eight?
When newborns came to them, were they surprised by their color as well as their sex?

Adam's name in Hebrew means dirt, soil, ground, or earth.
And when You created him, Abba, from the dust of the earth
You breathed life into his nostrils and made him a living soul.
Being a living soul made him different from the animals he would name.
So, was he a man of dark skin? Moses never said.

And Eve You made from Adam's rib and Adam said she was "bone of his bone."
He called her woman, and he was no longer alone.
So, was she fair because she was the color of his rib?
Perhaps I shouldn't ask but was she created with long hair or was she bald?
They were just two and created without preference or prejudice. So, how did that change?

What if when we conceive a child the infant's color was unknown until its birth?
Would a mother reject her newborn, a father not accept his child,
because when they looked at her or him, they saw a color that wasn't acceptable to them?
There have been babies born fair skinned to dark parents and dark skin to fair parents.
Biracial couples, not just dark and light, but mixed nationalities wait to see their baby's genetic blend.

How foolish Your children have become over color when it is only skin deep!
When I look in the mirror, I know what I see and what displeases me.
It really isn't my skin color, but things as equally as foolish.
I must confess aging is a problem I struggle with, and I color the gray in my hair.
And I've actually seen an albino man and he did look a little strange to me.

I remember when You sent Samuel out to anoint one of Jesse's sons to be Israel's next king.
When Samuel saw Eliab he said, "Certainly the Lord's anointed one is here before me."
*But You said to Samuel, **"Do not look at the appearance or stature of the man,***
Because I have rejected him. Man does not see what the LORD sees,
for man sees what is visible, but the LORD sees the heart." [1]

Now it is true I can't see a person's heart but do respond to their appearance.
Not just to their color, body shape, hair, or clothes, but to the appearance of the Spirit if living in them.
When the *Holy Spirit* is living inside of one of Your creations, *the Holy Spirit* living in me does respond.
Still, I confess, not all of Your children and I are friends, but I do seem to love them more readily.
Thankfully, my family and friends represent the best of the human DNA uniqueness You have created.

I know You love all of Your creation for You send Jesus to die for all our sins.
I understand that the indwelling of the Holy Spirit in each of Your elect is a special gift.
Adam, Eve, Abraham, Jacob, and Moses all saw You in some way.
Many saw Jesus when He lived among them, followed Him, and died for them.
What color did they see?

March 1, 2021

Abba, since You created us and Jesus came to save us by dying for us surely color should not be a weapon any longer for Satan to use to divide us. Rebuke Him, Abba, and heal us from this weakness. Grant us color blindness when it comes to our skin pigment. Forever Yours, Father, Son, and Holy Spirit – just as I am. Amen.

Choose Now Where You Will Spend Eternity

"I AM Yahweh, that is My name;
I will not give My glory to another or My praise to idols."
I created the universe, the solar systems, your planet and their laws.
You, mankind, were created as the human race, eternal beings because of Our love.
You are My greatest creation and I will never give up on restoring you to Us.

"I, I AM Yahweh, I alone declared, saved, and proclaimed —
And not some foreign god among you."
Oh, foolish child, place no man made gods or idols before Me, not even yourself.
I alone am sovereign so kings, judges, and governments are meaningless to Me.
I alone command armies of supernatural warrior angels.

"I AM Yahweh, and there is no other; there is no God but Me.
I will strengthen you, though you do not know Me."
But I want all of My creation to know Me as their sovereign Father.
I made you eternal beings that will gain eternal bodies when your mortal flesh ends.
Yes, you will go on living forever but must choose in life whether it is in heaven or hell.

I **AM** He who is your Divine Resident.
"Do you not know that you are My temple, the temple of God,
And that My Spirit dwells in you? If anyone defiles the temple of God,
I will destroy him. For the temple of God is holy, and you are that temple."
"Accept Jesus as your LORD and Savior, so My Holy Spirit may come and dwell in your heart."

I **AM, El Roi,** who sees and knows all that you think and do.
Know that you cannot separate what you do in your body – from your soul, mind, and spirit.
I have given you rules for your morality, purity and sexuality.
Do not grieve Me by following the world and seeking sexual pleasure outside My laws.
Is chasing after sexual desires in your body worth an eternity separated from Us?

I **AM** He who communicates with You.
Seek Our face and come close and listen when We speak.
When Elijah needed Us, the angel of the LORD came to him and gave him sustenance.
When I spoke to Elijah, My voice was not in the wind, or earthquake, or fire.
I engaged him in a still small voice, **"What are you doing here, Elijah."**

I **AM** sees you and knows you have made yourself god in My place.
You have allowed the lies of the Deceiver, Satan, to take root in you.
My child, you have forgotten that I alone am the Creator.
Angels bow in reverence to praise Me and obey My commands.
You disobey My commands when you become your own god choosing your plans over mine.

I **AM** reminds you that Satan lied to his fellow angels when they rebelled against me.
A third of my angels believed Satan's lies of equality within the Trinity.
They lost everything in the Rebellion and are destined to the eternal fires of hell.
Now he lies to you, for Satan seeks My creation, My children, to destroy them.
Turn to Jesus, seek salvation and escape the tempter's snare and fate.

I AM, knows you blame Me as your means to excuse your wayward desires.
You've said, "I am acceptable, for God made me this way."
When I created you, I gave you sexuality as a gift.
Like any gift, it is yours to use because I gave you freewill.
But I have given you commands to obey that govern all your choices, your sexuality.

I AM had Luke record in My Word, the Bible, the story of the Prodigal Son.
He took his inheritance, his Father's gifts, and squandered them.
He dishonored his father physically and morally with his body as you do Me.
Your body is not your own and your sexuality is for you to control according to My laws.
Return to Me and confess your sexual immortality for it grieves Me.

I AM aware of your other sins too including those of sexual promiscuousness.
I ordained marriage as a permanent lifetime relationship between one man and one woman.
Feeding your sexuality outside of marriage is not an unforgivable sin but sin, nonetheless.
Neither are the sins of homosexuality, abortion, racism, feminism, and transgenderism unforgiveable.
But you need to confess them to be forgiven and not repeat any action that offends Me.

I AM Immutable and Unchangeable. Do not place yourself above My laws.
"For I am the LORD, I do not change; therefore, you are not consumed."
"Jesus Christ, My only begotten Son, is the same yesterday, today, and forever."
"Every good gift and every perfect gift is from above, and comes down to you from Me.
I AM the Father of lights, with whom there is no variation or shadow of turning."

I AM has destroyed people groups for transgressing My laws.
All sexual sin, abortion, racism, feminism, transgenderism offends Me.
Homosexuality is a perversion of the sexuality of My greatest creation, man.
Do not believe the lie that My ancient laws governing your life have changed.
Are you better than your ancestors? Better than Jesus who came to fulfill the laws?

I AM asks you a question. Stand still and answer me.
Do you not know that I am unapproachable by My children when they are tainted by sin?
I cannot allow any sin or unrepented child into Paradise.
So, child, what can you possess or do that is worth eternal separation from Me?
Dear one, your mortal flesh will end and you will gain an immortal body that will live forever.

I AM asks you to search your heart and mind for wisdom.
Would you swallow poison and die?
Would you choose any sin, or please your perverted sexual nature for your limited mortal life?
Think I AM is not real? Think that Satan isn't ruling your world into chaos?
Teaching tolerance of sin sounds loving and right to a corrupt man but it is a lie.

I AM requires the choice of your eternal destination be made before your mortal body dies.
It is foolish to please your mortal desires now believing you'll have time to confess before you die.
So, what in your mortal life is worth eternity in hell?
Come to Me child, confess your sins and I will forgive you and blot them out and remember them no more.
You can start fresh and I will guide you to your eternal life in the Heavenlies.

I AM *the Judge of the world I created.*
"Now there is no condemnation for those who are in
Christ Jesus, because through Him, the law of the Spirit,
Has set you free from the law of sin and death."
All those who come to Us through My Son, Jesus, will live eternally with Us.

I AM, Jesus, the Founder and Perfecter of your faith.
"Who for the joy set before Me endured the cross,
Despising the shame of crucifixion to meet your needs,
And I AM seated at the right hand of the throne of My Father."
Loving you, I was crucified in your place, so what good would I withhold from you?

I AM Jesus your Savior. The Living One. Your Deliverer.
"I paid for your citizenship in heaven.
I will transform your mortal body to be like My glorious body,
By the power of the Father that enables Me to subject all things to Myself.
And Our Holy Spirit indwells you to be your Counselor, Comforter, and Guide home."

I AM your Advocate and I sit at the right hand of the Father.
Our Holy Spirit living inside of you is there to guide you so listen to Him.
When you sin, I will advocate for you with the Father.
Come to Us; confess your sin that is covered by My blood; and We will forgive your sin.
Do not make a habit of sinning and confessing – live righteously through Us.

I AM the Living Word.
"For the word of God is living and active.
My word is sharper than any two-edged sword, piercing to the division of soul and spirit,
Of joints and of marrow and <u>discerning </u>the thoughts and intentions of the heart.
"Study and know My Word. Continue in My Word and it will set you free."

I AM King Jesus and I am returning soon to secure My own.
"But concerning that day and hour no one knows, not even the angels in heaven.
*Nor even I, the Son, but the Father only until He says, "**Son, gather Our children!**"*
"Therefore, be ready, for I am coming at an hour you do not expect.
For your perishable body must put on the imperishable, and your mortal body immortality."

Choose eternal life in Me, my child, for anything less means eternal suffering!

August 28, *Issues Dividing America* sermon by Dave Early

Abba, thank you for another piece that matches what is happening in our world. Abba, bring revival for it is all that will spare us now from a world order we do not want. Prepare our children and grandchildren to treat their bodies as a worthy place for the Holy Spirit to live. We are greatly concerned for the confusing messages they are hearing. Holy Spirit, show them the truth; give them the wisdom to reject the lies and half-truths they are hearing; teach them to hear only you and be dependent on you. We cannot protect them. Show them a way out of their lifestyle choices and make them pure again. In Jesus' Holy Name. Your world without end, Abba, forever and always. Amen.

Conclusion
Life and Death

"In the same way, count yourselves dead to sin but alive to God in Christ Jesus." [1]

Life and death are covered in the same sentence. But being dead is directed toward sin and life is directed to God through our Savior Jesus Christ. We die to sin by accepting the free gift of salvation offered to us by Christ. Jesus paid our debt of sin and when we ask for forgiveness, He stamps our debt ledger "Paid in Full."

Done. We are free of sin. Not perfect, so when we sin, we need to seek forgiveness yet again, but Christ's perfect sacrifice covers all our sin—even those we have yet to commit. The good news is we don't live in a spiraling cycle of sin and forgiveness. With the *Holy Spirit* living in us as our helper, we can know God's truth, act on it, avoid temptation and bad choices, and live and grow. We can prepare our souls for eternal life—our true destiny in Christ.

Who is our Helper sent by Christ? He is the third person of the Holy Trinity. This Holy Spirit is our guide, our comforter, leader in truth, and He is on duty 24/7. Artists have rendered their inspired versions of Christ. Because He came in human flesh, we can think of Him in human form, although no one in His time on earth captured His image for us. And, God, being His Father and ours, we can imagine as a physical being.

But how do we picture the Holy Spirit? In **"God said, Let us make man in our own image."** [2] God was speaking to His son Jesus and the Holy Spirit. The Holy Spirit was sent to us in the New Testament, but He was there in the Godhead from the beginning. [3]

The Hebrew word for Spirit is *'ruwach'* which means breath, wind, or spirit. The Greek word is pneuma which means vital spirit, creative force, or spirit of truth. It is only fitting then to see the Holy Spirit as our breath, the wind beneath our wings. The Greek is exciting too because pneuma is used medically for lung related things and it refers to the whole process of our vascular system which carries oxygen throughout our bodies. Vital force, creative force, and spirit of truth all make perfect sense and Spirit of Truth is used in the Bible referring to the Holy Spirit. Vital force to me means living force. I like the thought that the Holy Spirit is a creative force reshaping us in the image of the Trinity for eternal life with them in heaven.

So, I think we reflect the Trinity—physically and spiritually. *"And the LORD God formed man from the dust of the ground and breathed into his nostrils the <u>breath of life</u>: and man became a living soul."* [4]

So, we are physical as well as spiritual beings just like our Creator. There is no clearer or more beautiful picture of the Trinity then when John baptized Christ. **"As soon as Jesus was baptized, He went up out of the water. At that moment heaven was opened, and He saw the Spirit of God descending like a dove and alighting on Him. And a voice from heaven said, "This is my Son, whom I love; with Him I am well pleased."** [5]

Here the veil between heaven and earth is opened and God speaks, the Holy Spirit descends in the form of a dove, as our Savior emerges from the water. Play a video in your head—the Shekinah Glory of God spilling out of a split in the heavens, a supernatural white dove descending from heaven and alighting on Christ's shoulder and our precious Christ coming out of the Jordan.

There is a God-shaped void in each of us which can only be filled by the Spirit of God. We are incomplete without Him taking His rightful place in us. Our spiritual being is incomplete without the third member of the Trinity living inside of us reshaping us into the image of Jesus Christ, God's Son.

Our earthly physical being can exist outside the unity we were designed to have with the Trinity. Much like a trauma victim can be kept alive on a respirator, so the unsaved can spend their days relying on the physical world to sustain them. Then, death takes the unsaved to "the lake of fire" created for the punishment of demons who gather the unsaved to share their fate.

Our mortal bodies weren't designed to last forever, and the world is not destined to remain restrained and traumatized by sin. So, my body will, one day, cease to sustain me, but because I am *"alive to God in Christ Jesus"* [6] a new body awaits me that is not made by human hands. [7] Then my real forever life will begin, and I won't be alone for all Christ has gathered will be there. I will be reunited with loved ones waiting there for me, and I will meet ones I never knew. I will live among the people of the Bible whose lives guided mine. I will be home because the Holy Spirit living inside of me will guide me there.

Each of us are eternal beings that will one day take on an eternal body to house our eternal soul. We will recognize each other in our best whole form, not aged or impaired. *For now, we see in a mirror, dimly, but then face to face. Now I know in part, but then I shall know just as I also am known.* [8]

Someday time will be complete for the world too and a new earth will replace the one worn out. *"Now I saw a new heaven and a new earth, for the first heaven and the first earth had passed away. Also, there was no more sea. Then I, John, saw the holy city, New Jerusalem, coming down out of heaven from God, prepared as a bride adorned for her husband. And I heard a loud voice from heaven saying, "Behold, the tabernacle of God is with men, and He will dwell with them, and they shall be His people. God Himself will be with them and be their God. And God will wipe away every tear from their eyes; there shall be no more death, nor sorrow, nor crying. There shall be no more pain, for the former things have passed away."* [9]

Then, I will live in the presence of God, and He will give me a new name. ***"And I will give him a white stone, and on the stone a new name written which no one knows except him who receives it."*** [10]

Has your God-shaped void been filled with the Holy Spirit?
Where will you spend eternity? Heaven or Hell?

Gracious Father I scarce can take it in. I confess that I do not understand all that is the Trinity. But I know that Christ came from that Unity, suffered death for me as an atonement for my sins, and was restored to it. I understand Your plan for me to someday leave behind the temporary and come to live with You permanently. To live in the Eternal City described in Revelation that I can't even imagine. But my imagination isn't required for You have already designed it. Thank you for giving me eternal life and a room in the Eternal City. In Jesus' Holy Name. Amen. September 30, 2016

Introduction to Faith in Jesus

In the beginning God created the universe, and all His creation was good. In the midst of His great work, He created a garden, and in it He created a man, Adam, who He breathed life into, and from the man's rib, He created a woman, Eve. They were given dominion over the garden and were satisfied.

God, their Creator, visited with them in the garden and they walked together in the cool of the evening in pleasant fellowship and love. They could eat any of the fruits from the garden except the fruit from the Tree of the Knowledge of Good and Evil. Only this was withheld from them, as God knew it would overwhelm them and bring sin into the Garden Beautiful.

The Creator of the universe created messengers to serve Him and they were called angels. One of them, a beautiful angel named Lucifer (meaning bright and morning star) felt himself equal to God and a great war in heaven ended in his fall from service and one-third of the angels in heaven went with him. After their Rebellion, Lucifer became known as Satan (meaning astray and adversary—a malevolent entity who deceives mankind), and the fallen angels who served him were called demons.

One day in this Beautiful garden of light, love, and satisfaction called _Eden_ the malevolent shadow of darkness came. The malevolent shadow entered a lovely creature, a serpent, to deceive Eve. Now, Eve saw that the fruit of the Tree of the Knowledge of Good and Evil was pleasant to look at and knew that like all the other fruit in Eden that it would be good to taste. So, the Serpent lied to the woman saying that God was withholding the fruit from her and Adam, because God did not want them to become as powerful and all-knowing as He was.

So, being deceived by the Serpent, Eve tasted the fruit and grew in the knowledge of good and evil. Then, she gave the fruit to Adam, who on his own accord, ate the forbidden fruit forbidden to them. But they were not as powerful and not as all-knowing as God and the man and the woman were ashamed, miserable, and no longer satisfied.

God came to walk with them in the cool of the evening after their disobedience, but now having the knowledge of good and evil, Adam and Eve hid from their loving Creator. And because of their disobedience, sin and death entered the world.

Now God was not surprised by their disobedience, but it did sadden Him. Still, He loved His beautiful children, and so placed into action the plan that would give them a choice to be restored to fellowship with Him. Sadly though, they could no longer live in Eden because in the garden the Tree of Life grew and gave them immortality, and they could not continue to eat from this tree and live in Eden with their corrupt spirits and bodies.

So, the plan of salvation and restoration was fulfilled when God's only Son left the throne room of heaven, and came to earth as the tiny infant, Jesus Christ. He walked the earth as God and _Man_ for thirty-three years, and for three of those years He taught His disciples the plan of salvation by which man can be reconciled to God.

Then Jesus Christ became our sacrifice for the plan of salvation could not be free. Christ paid the cost to cover sin once and for all on the cross of Calvary, freely giving His life for ours. Oh, but death did not win for although He gave up His life, _He_ took it up again in just three days. So, Jesus Christ became our Redeemer removing the sting of death for any who would believe.

Then, Christ our Beloved Savior returned to the Father's throne from where God sent the Holy Spirit to not just live with us on earth as did Christ, but to live in us and so teach us to glory in the Creator day by day as we sojourn on this earthly plain.

We, beloved, have a God shaped void in us, put there by the Father so we would seek Him, the Christ, and the Holy Spirit. You may try to deny it. You may try to fill it with drugs, alcohol, sex, worldly games and distractions, but nothing can satisfy the God shape void in you, until you ask for the forgiveness paid by Jesus Christ crucified.

You can do nothing to earn this gift of salvation and restoration with God, for Christ already paid the full cost and shares it freely to all who ask. All you can bring to Christ is yourself and your sin, and Christ's blood will wash away your sin, and you then will live whole in Him.

Once asked, the gift comes. You are restored. Then, you will walk with Christ and your journey on earth will have meaning. You will be complete and never willingly disobey or sin again. Then one day the plan of restoration will be complete for you. You will leave this earth behind and take up your immortal glorified body and live forever with God.

There is a battle for your soul, beloved. A battle to where you will spend eternity. Christ would have you spend eternity in His light in heaven, the new garden, where sin may never again come. The Holy Spirit and angels will fight to give you this knowledge of forgiveness and life. Satan and his demons will fight to have you spend eternity in the eternal fires prepared just for them.

Do not be deceived, beloved. Hell is a real place. It was not prepared for the beloved, but for Satan, demons, and those deceived by the lies of the malevolent spirits. Seek grace and the truth. Seek light.

You are on your own journey and your life touches many others. I pray you will complete your journey to Christ. He died so you would not suffer the spiritual death of separation from the Eternal.

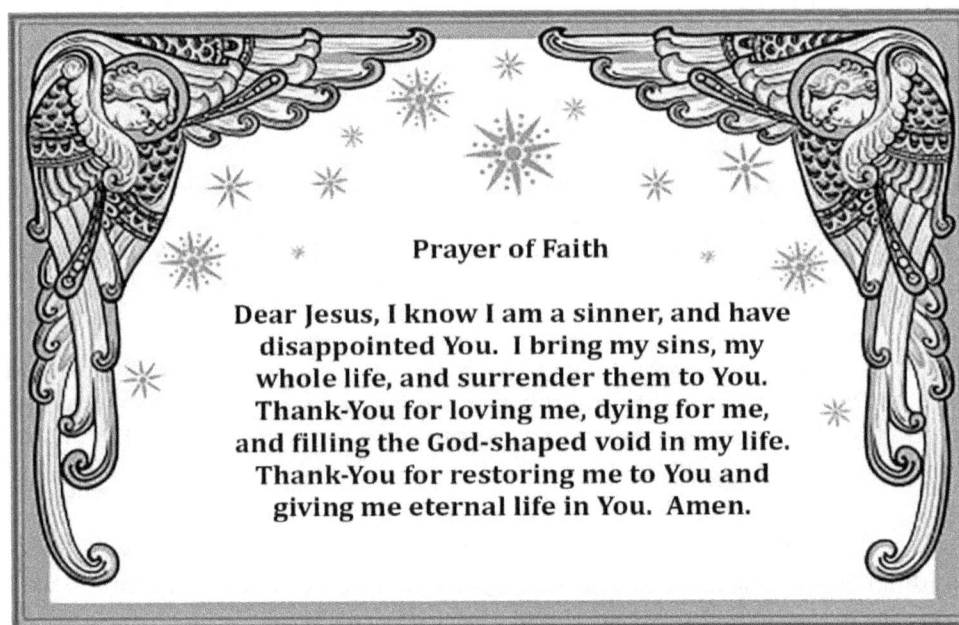

Prayer of Faith

Dear Jesus, I know I am a sinner, and have disappointed You. I bring my sins, my whole life, and surrender them to You. Thank-You for loving me, dying for me, and filling the God-shaped void in my life. Thank-You for restoring me to You and giving me eternal life in You. Amen.

What now?

If you prayed this prayer, take a minute and rest in the comfort of the Triune presence. There are over forty-two hundred religions, and you don't need to practice a religion, but worship and serve in a body of believers in Jesus. I would recommend a local Southern Baptist Church, but let the Holy Spirit lead you to a body of believers that will help you grow.

About the Author

      With sixty-nine years of experience, I am grateful for love and the gifts of love given without packages, bows, or cards. God's love provided for my salvation, family, marriage, children, grandchildren, and my friends. I am a disciple of Christ practicing my faith daily amongst other Southern Baptists. I have two very adult children and seven additional blessings, my grandchildren. I am a retired widow with degrees in medical laboratory technology and communication. I have a developing interest in alternative medicine, essential oils, supplements, herbs, and cell salts which God provides for us for our good.

      I believe in our Creator's designs for our bodies and spirits and their ability to heal given what they need. I enjoy Bible studies with my Christian lady friends. I share teaching ELL (English Language Learners) with a number of other church members. Although I learned the mechanics of writing from teachers, the characters and their stories come from the Holy Spirit. My characters share the lessons of the Spirit I have been taught. Writing through the Holy Spirit is food for my soul, the air I breathe, and a fire in my bones that I desire to share.

Books by Rhoda Fegan

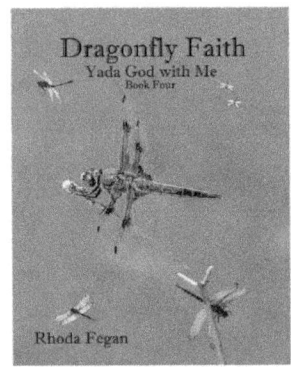

All books are available at www.Amazon.com

Notes

I have attempted to footnote the scriptures in my poems. To footnote a poem is an unusual undertaking but I want you to know that they are from the Bible and I pray that I have captured them correctly. If not, I plead human, google the scripture and find its true source. I have not forged any line to sound like scripture. BibleGateway is a favorite tool of mine.

Scriptures references come from various sources but I prefer the NKJV and New American Standard Translation, The Ryrie Study Bible 1978 The Moody Bible Institute of Chicago (my favorite personal Bible). Some verses are not recorded as written but more in conversational form when used as such in a piece. Scripture is initialized and scripture spoken by God or Jesus is italicized and bolded. Remember to verify for yourself the scriptures for the content of these pieces.

Introduction

[1] Stickney, Doris "Waterbugs and Dragonflies : Explaining Death to Young Children", New York City, Pilgrim Press 1982.

Chapter One: Good Friday Offerings

Sting

[1] Luke 22:62   [2] Luke 23:32-43   [3] Luke 23:44-49   [4] Luke 27:45-54
[5] Luke 2:19   [6] Luke 2:39-52   [7] John 19:25-29   [8] Psalm 119:11
[9] 1 Corinthians 15:54-56

Bruised, Bloodied, But Not Broken

[1] Matthew 27:46   [2] John 19:30   [3] Luke 22:42,   Mark 14:36

Eternal Beings
[1] Ecclesiastes 3:11

Redemption's Glorious Plan
[1] Zechariah 9:9   [4] Luke 23:33-43
[2] Mark 14:32-42   [5] Matthew 27:46
[3] John 18:1-13   [6] John 19:28-30

The Betrothal
[1] Genesis 1-2   [4] Revelation 21
[2] Genesis 3   [5] John 17:2, 10:28
[3] 2 Corinthians 5:1   [6] 2 Corinthians 1:22

Road to Emmaus
[1] Luke 24:13-27   [2] Luke 10:1-11   [3] John 20:11-18   [4] Luke 24:19   [5] Luke 24:25-26
[6] Luke 24:27   [7] Luke 24:30-31   [8] Luke 24:32   [9] Luke 24:33-35   [10] Luke 24:36-49

Jesus, "I AM"

[1] John 18:1-11   [2] Luke 4:30   [3] Matthew 26:53-56   [4] John 13:27
[5] Exodus 3:14   [6] Romans 14:11 Isaiah 45:23   [7] John 14:6   [8] John 10:9
[9] Exodus 12:23   [10] Matthew 27:50-53   [11] John 10:7-11   [12] John 20:24-29

His Words

[1] Luke 23:34   [2] Luke 23:43   [3] John 19:25-27   [4] Matthew 27:46
[5] Luke 23:46   [6] John 19:28-30   [7] Acts 1:8

The Tomb and the Stone

[1] John 19:28-30   [2] John 20:1-18   [3] John 3:16   [4] Mark 16

Unstoppable Love

[1] Genesis 6:9-9:17   [2] Genesis 12-25   [3] Genesis 37:2-50:26   [4] Matthew 1:1-17, Luke 3:23-38
[5] 2 Samuel 7:11-16   [6] Revelation 22:16   [7] Jeremiah 31:15, Matthew 2:18   [8] Matthew 3
[9] Matthew 4:1-11   [10] Psalm 91:11-13   [11] 1 John 2:15-17   [12] 1 Corinthians 10:13
[13] Luke 6:12-16   [14] Matthew 21:1-9, Mark 11:1-10, Luke 19: 28-39, John 12: 12-18
[15] Matthew 26:17-30, Luke 22:7-38, Mark 14:12-31   [16] John 17   [17] Matthew 26, Luke 22
[18] Hebrews 5:7   [19] Hebrews 12:2   [20] Luke 22, Matthew 26, John 18   [21] Luke 4:28-30
[22] John 7:30   [23] Matthew 26:53-56   [24] Luke 23, Matthew 26, John 19   [25] Psalm 22
[26] John 19:26-17   [27] Luke 23:39-43   [28] Matthew 27:46   [29] John 19:28-30
[30] Matthew 27:51-54   [31] John 19:31-37   [32] Number 9:12   [33] John 19, Zechariah 12:10
[34] Zechariah 12:10   [35] Mark 15:43   [36] John 3 and 7   [37] John 19, Matthew 27:57-60
[38] Mark 8:31   [39] Revelation 1:18   [40] Matthew 28:1-4   [41] Matthew 28:11-15
[42] Matthew 28:5-8   [43] Matthew 26:32, Mark 14:28   [44] Matthew 28:16-20   [45] Luke 22:17-20
[46] Revelation 21:1-4

Do not love the world or the things in the world. If anyone loves the world,
the love of the Father is not in him.
For all that is in the world – the desires of the flesh and the desires
of the eyes and pride in possessions – is not from the Father but is from the world.
And the world is passing away along with its desires, but whoever does the will of God abides forever.
1 John 2:15-17

The Wilderness, The Garden, The Cross, and The Borrowed Tomb

[1] Revelation 13:8   [10] John 18:10   [19] John 19:30   [28] Mark 16:20
[2] Matthew 4:3-11   [11] John 18:11   [20] Matthew 27:51   [29] Acts 1:9-12
[3] Luke 4:14   [12] Matthew 26:53   [21] Mark 8:31   [30] 1 Corinthians 15:55
[4] John 8:32   [13] Luke 22:51   [22] Isaiah 53:9   [31] John 8:36
[5] Mark 14:36   [14] Isaiah 50:6   [23] 1 Peter 3:18
[6] Luke 22:43   [15] Isaiah 52:14   [24] Mark 16:3
[7] Matthew 26:49   [16] Luke 23:34   [25] Matthew 28:1-8
[8] John 18:6   [17] Psalm 22:1 Matthew 27:46   [26] John 20:15-18
[9] Luke 22:49   [18] Luke 23:46   [27] Mark 16:15-16

Jesus our Messiah

[1] Revelation 13:8 [6] Genesis 7 [11] Genesis 40, 41:1-45 [16] Joshua 6
[2] Genesis 5:24 [7] Genesis 16:16 [12] Genesis 38 [17] Ruth
[3] Genesis 9:11-13 [8] Genesis 39:4 [13] Genesis 44,45:1-3 [18] 1 Chronicles 2:12-15
[4] Genesis 12:1-3 [9] Genesis 39:9 [14] Genesis 45:4-8 [19] 2 Samuel 7:12-17
[5] Genesis 15:1 and 5 [10] Genesis 40:15 [15] Joshua 2 and 5 [20] 2 Samuel 12:24, 5:14

The Temple Veil and Saints Resurrected

[1] Luke 23:44 [8] Hebrews 9:11-12 [15] Revelation 1:7 [22] John 12:42-43
[2] Matthew 27:46b [9] Hebrews 9:13 [16] Matthew 27:54
[3] Luke 23:45 [10] John 14:6 [17] Luke 2:34-25
[4] Matthew 27:50-51 [11] Numbers 9:12 [18] Matthew 27:50-53
[5] John 19:28-30 [12] John 19:31-34 [19] 1 Corinthians 15:20-22
[6] Luke 23:46 [13] Psalm 34:20 [20] John 5:28-29
[7] John 19:30 [14] Zechariah 12:10 [21] Romans 2:6-9,11

Chapter Two: Christmas Offerings

King Jesus, Abide in Him

[1] Micah 4:8, 5:2 [2] John 19:30 [3] Matthew 28:16-20

Eternal Covenant Keeper

[1] Genesis Creation 1:1-2-7 [16] Saul king 1 Samuel 9, 16:14
[2] Genesis 2:20-25 [17] 1 Samuel 16:1-13
[3] Genesis 3:1-16 [18] 2 Samuel 7:12-16, Jeremiah 33:17
[4] Genesis 3:17-24 [19] 1 Sam 13:14; Acts 13:22
[5] Genesis 4:1-2 [20] 1 Kings 11:1-13
[6] Genesis 4:3-16 [21] 1Kings 11:43, 1Kings 12:1-3
[7] Genesis 4:25-26 [22] Lineage of Joseph Matthew 1:1-17
[8] Genesis 5:1-9:28 Lineage of Mary Luke 3:23-38
[9] Genesis 11:10-26 [23] Luke 1:26-33
[10] Genesis 15-16, 21- 22 [24] Luke 2:25-35, 1 John 2:1-2
[11] Genesis 25:1-11 [25] Hebrews 7:25, 9:24, 1 Timothy 2:5
[12] Joseph Genesis 37-47 [26] John 10:28
[13] Moses and the Exodus, Exodus 1-12 [27] Revelation 1:7
[14] Ten Commandments – Exodus 20, [28] Jeremiah 31: 31-34, Hebrews 8:10-12
40-year sojourn Numbers 14:28-34
Death of Moses Deuteronomy 34:1-12
[15] Caleb Joshua 14:6-14

Remember Me"

[1] Matthew 16:23
[2] Luke 22:15-16
[3] Matthew 26:20-25
[4] Luke 22:32
[5] Luke 22:14-20
[6] Revelation 5:9-10
[7] Matthew 28, Mark 16, Luke 24, John 20
[8] Matthew 26:26-28

Chapter Three: Praise and Worship

Absolutely

[1] Philippians 4:6
[2] Philippians 4:13

Jesus Our Veteran

[1] Luke 9:28-36

Elohim

[1] "We are hard pressed on every side, <u>but not</u> crushed; perplexed, <u>but not</u> in despair; persecuted, <u>but not</u> abandoned; struck down, <u>but not</u> destroyed." 2 Corinthians 4:8
[2] The Spirit and the bride say, "Come!" And let the one who hears say, "Come!" Let the one who is thirsty come; and let the one who wishes take the free gift of the water of life COME. Revelation 22:17.

We are Yours

[1] Hebrews 12:2	[2] Genesis 1:26	[3] Genesis 2:7	[4] Genesis 2:21-24
[5] Isaiah 64:8	[6] Psalm 27:8	[7] Deuteronomy 4:29	[8] Jeremiah 29:11
[9] Jeremiah 29:12-13	[10] Jeremiah 32:17-18a	[11] Jeremiah 33:3	[12] Isaiah 43:2
[13] Isaiah 41:10	[14] Proverbs 18:10	[15] Psalm 91:1	[16] Psalms 91:3-6
[17] Isaiah 40:6-8	[18] Psalms 91:14-16	[19] Psalms 94:19	[20] Isaiah 40:12-15
[21] Isaiah 40:22-26	[22] Isaiah 40:28	[23] John 3:16-18	[24] Isaiah 40:29-31
[25] Matthew 11:28-30	[26] Matthew 28:18:20	[27] John 14:1-6	[28] John 14:27
[29] John 15:11-12	[30] Philippians 4:4-6	[31] Philippians 4:7	[32] Philippians 4:13
[33] Ecc 3:11	[34] 2 Timothy 1:7	[35] Mark 9:24	[36] Matthew 26:28
[37] John 10:28-30	[38] Psalm 56:3	[39] Psalm 121:4, Isaiah 28	[40] Romans 8:31
[41] Romans 8:35, 37-39	[42] Michal 7:7-8	[43] Zephaniah 3:17	[44] Psalm 37:4-5
[45] Joshua 1:9	[46] Habakkuk 3:18		

What God Seeks from Us

Deuteronomy
[1] 4:2	[2] 4:29	[3] 4:30-3	[4] 5:7-21	[5] 6:5	[6] 6:14	[7] 6-18
[8] 8:3	[9] 8:1	[10] 11:1	[11] 11:13-17	[12] 11:18-23	[13] 12:28-32	[14] 13:2-4
[15] 14:22	[16] 15:10	[17] 16:17	[18] 6:19-20	[19] 17:18-20	[20] 22:5	[21] 24:14-20
[22] 30:6	[23] 30:6,9-11, 14-16		[24] 31:6, 8	[25] 33:12	[26] 34:26, 29	

Chapter Four: The Trinity Calling

Unconditional Forgiveness

[1] Psalm 103:12
[2] John 14:27

Come to Me

[1] Matthew 11:28-30
[2] John 14:27
[3] Isaiah 40:31
[4] Isaiah 45:2
[5] John 10:28
[6] John 14:1
[7] 1 Peter 5:7
[8] Psalm 46:1-3, Matthew 28:20

Forgiveness is Letting Go

[1] Matthew 18:22
[2] Luke 23:34
[3] Luke 23:34

Color

[1] I Samuel 16

Conclusion: Life and Death

[1] Romans 6:11
[2] Genesis 1:26a
[3] Genesis 1:2
[4] Genesis 2:7
[5] Matthew 3:16-17
[6] Romans 6:11
[7] 2 Corinthians 5:1
[8] 1 Corinthians 13:12
[9] Revelation 21:1-4
[10] Revelation 2:17

www.ingramcontent.com/pod-product-compliance
Lightning Source LLC
LaVergne TN
LVHW081316060426
835509LV00015B/1537